MICROCARS

TONY MARSHALL

SUTTON PUBLISHING LIMITED

Sutton Publishing Limited
Phoenix Mill · Thrupp · Stroud
Gloucestershire · GL5 2BU

First published 1999

British Library Cataloguing in Publication Data
A catalogue record for this book is available from the
British Library.

ISBN 0-7509-2083-2

Typeset in 10.5/13.5 Photina.
Typesetting and origination by
Sutton Publishing Limited.
Printed in Great Britain by
Ebenezer Baylis, Worcester.

This book is dedicated to the memory of Edwin Hammond, a true enthusiast. Let him be remembered wherever microcars are enjoyed.

Edwin Hammond, 1930–1999.

CONTENTS

ACKNOWLEDGEMENTS

Before compiling this page, my first thought was to wonder whether people actually read the acknowledgements or whether they simply skip the first few pages and plunge headlong into the nitty-gritty of photographs and text. First of all, therefore, I would like to thank you, the reader, for taking the time and trouble not only to look between the covers, but also to study the finer print.

No book of this sort could be produced without the cars first having been built, so thanks are inevitably due to those entrepreneurs, businessmen, craftsmen (and women) and others who have been involved through the years making the cars discussed on these pages. We should not forget, also, those with the foresight to record what took place, achieving such splendid results with relatively primitive cameras and film.

So many people have been so helpful with the supply of material for publication that someone will almost inevitably be omitted from the list. Please forgive any such oversight on my part. The bulk of the illustrations, not to mention encouragement, came from Jean and Edwin Hammond who founded the Register of Unusual Microcars – Edwin tragically passed away while the final text was being prepared, but Jean retains her microcar involvement. Without contributions from Mike Shepherd, Martin Boddy – Bond Bug Club, Stan Cornock – Bond Minicar Owners' Club, Bob Neal – Reliant Owners' Club, Michael Russell, Norman Gillard, D.A.T. Grimmett, Walter Zeichner in Germany and Antoní Tacho in Spain, the helpful people at the Priaulx Library in Guernsey, Laurence Jeavons and Fred Diwell in Australia, Wynford Jones – Messerschmitt Owners' Club, Dave Watson – Isetta Owners' Club of Great Britain, Gilbert Jepson, Gavin Allard, Otto and Marianne Kunnecke (a visit to their Automuseum Störy in Germany is essential for any serious enthusiast of microcars), Derek Merkelt, Stephen Boyd – Scootacar Register, Alastair Cave, Steve Fay, Brian Madeley – Mechanical Horse Club, Mrs Doreen Davies, Mike Webster, Malcolm Thomas, Malcolm Goldsworthy, Jim Boulton and Colin Corke this book would have been a sorry document indeed. Norbert Mylius deserves a special mention for supplying not only photographs but also a wealth of information about the Felber.

It is a pleasure also to mention my wife Lynne, without whose computer the task would have been far more onerous, and without whose help I would be floundering under a sea of paper. The computer and I have a relationship based upon mutual distrust, so I grudgingly acknowledge the part it has played – even though it nearly drove me to despair on several occasions. Kim Lowden encouraged from afar and researched odd details on my behalf from the 'wrong' side of the Atlantic Ocean so promptly that she will probably be asked to do more of the same, should I be granted another opportunity to inscribe my name on a book cover. Michael Worthington Williams, Malcolm McKay and Chris Rees, motoring writers whose credentials I can only aspire to, have been both helpful and encouraging to a beginner – thank you, gentlemen, for the above and for your help with pictures.

Finally, thank you Simon and Annabel at Sutton Publishing for having faith in my efforts, and for making so many scraps of paper come together so satisfactorily in the form of a book.

INTRODUCTION

'What – no Heinkel?', may well be the cry as readers flick through this book. Many will be dismayed to find their own favourite microcar omitted, and for this the author apologises. To include everyone's favourite would be an impossible task, given the format and number of pages. It was decided at an early stage that to provide a balanced content it was desirable to include examples of both the better known and the more obscure microcars, and to do that meant omitting some that really did deserve to be included. Some makes (not the Heinkel) more or less de-selected themselves simply because reliable sources of suitable material were not able to assist, whereas other less-known makes have not been documented elsewhere despite the availability of a wealth of material and these, surely, merit space. It is to be hoped that, subject to this volume being well received, Sutton Publishing Ltd will provide an opportunity to redress the balance. So look out all those old photographs in readiness – they may turn out to be vital to the inclusion of your favourite make and model on a future occasion.

The term 'microcar' is an assumed one with no basis in officialese. For this reason it cannot be defined with complete certainty, and the question of just what constitutes a microcar is one that can be discussed at length without ever reaching a clear conclusion. For the purpose of simplicity this book will follow the most commonly held view that microcars are vehicles built after the end of the Second World War, usually with economy of construction and of use as the main criteria. Microcars can have either three wheels or four, and power is usually provided by an internal combustion engine, though battery electric propulsion is not unknown. Where petrol is the fuel, the engines are often of the two-stroke type which, with fewer parts, are less expensive to produce. Most manufacturers of microcars tended to use power units that were already in production for other applications, with or without modification. The maximum engine displacement for a microcar is generally agreed to be 700 cc. Certain microcars also fall under the generic term 'bubble cars'. This is a self-explanatory term dating from the 1950s when these cars – principally the Messerschmitt, Heinkel (later Trojan), and Isetta – were available new, and derives from the rounded design styles and large window areas of the vehicles. Hence, bubble cars all come under the heading of microcars, but the reverse is less often the case.

The origin of the term microcar cannot be verified but the author believes it came about in the following manner. Back in the 1960s and '70s interest in and enthusiasm for odd-looking economy cars, often with strange single-cylinder engines emitting the characteristic blue two-stroke haze from the exhaust, and fewer than the conventional four wheels, was at a very low ebb. Just a small number of individualistic – and frequently impecunious – stalwart owners were prepared to be seen out and about with their vehicles. Admittedly there were owners' clubs even then. Those for the Berkeley, Bond and Messerschmitt marques did remarkably well in anticipating later developments, and deserve much credit for the survival of so many microcars into the more appreciative world that enjoys them so many years later. But microcars, mostly already well beyond their anticipated life-spans, were perceived as objects of derision, and their owners as eccentrics, deemed worthy of little short of ridicule. In this atmosphere, in 1975, took place an event that was publicised as a 'Multi-make Three-Wheeler Rally'. The Cotswold Wildlife Park at Burford was selected as the venue for this rally, the success of which may be gauged by the fact that it subsequently developed into an annual jamboree for microcar owners throughout Britain as well as enthusiasts from overseas, and has played a large part in the growth of the microcar movement for more than two decades. However, the first rally having taken place, it became obvious that by restricting participating vehicles to a tricycle form a further group of vehicles sharing so many other characteristics with the three wheelers was being unfairly excluded. Discussion at a local meeting of the Messerschmitt Owners' Club at Forest Row in Sussex threw up the suggested term 'microcar'. Nobody has ever been credited with this stroke of genius but, the vagaries of memory aside, it seems likely to have been voiced first by Andrew Woolley – an enthusiast then, and now.

How strange that some of the keenest of present-day enthusiasts for cars with an anticipated life-span of, perhaps, six to eight years, were not even born at the time of that first rally. . . .

CHAPTER ONE

PRE-WAR ORIGINS: POST-WAR INNOVATIONS

Lightweight economy vehicles have been produced since the dawning of the age of the motor car. Usually they have remained strictly on the side-lines, receiving scant attention from press or public. Occasionally, and particularly following times of major conflict when manpower has suddenly become available in large numbers and industry has been bolstered by a period of production at full capacity to maintain the war effort, but also subjected to acute shortages of traditional materials, these little cars have come into their own. Such a time occurred in the second half of the 1940s.

Reliant had been making three-wheeled vans before the war. Lloyd had been constructing cars to their own design since 1936. Both recommenced as soon as circumstances permitted, though Lloyd's post-war design, announced in 1946 and in production from 1948, was all new and had more in common with conventional cars than microcars. They were joined by newcomers including Bond, whose creation was an ultra-lightweight and very simplified three-wheeler that proved highly successful. Lloyd failed to compete successfully and subsequently abandoned car manufacture. Reliant recognised the opportunity and introduced their own three-wheeled car in aluminium, then fibreglass, going on to become one of the mainstays of the British motor industry during a period when other makers were succumbing to foreign imports.

The Reliant name has become a household word, not just because the company has been producing vehicles for over sixty years, not simply because it is one of the few remaining independent British motor manufacturers, but also because the cars bearing the name Reliant have been the object of a great many jokes. The Reliant story, however, is far from being a laughing matter, as generations of satisfied owners, faithful to the marque, will affirm.

The first Reliant products were actually descended from those of the Raleigh Cycle Company of Nottingham. Raleigh produced a three-wheeled car called the Safety Seven from 1933.

A Raleigh Safety Seven of 1934. They were never particularly numerous but one example is reputed to have been owned for a short time by the author's father. Regrettably the author was born too late to enjoy personal experience of this fascinating vehicle.

The Raleigh Company also made a commercial van, but this had a very different appearance, with the front wheel and forks outside the boxy van body. The style was not dissimilar to vans from the A.J. Stevens and James motorcycle companies, but the Raleigh designs were the original work of Raleigh in-house designer T.L. Williams.

This photograph of a gathering of the *Raleigh Safety Seven* and *Early Reliant Club* at the Reliant works, probably in the early 1970s, shows a brace of Safety Seven cars, and a very early commercial (on the bed of the Transit truck) in the company of 6-cwt Reliants and, beyond the pair of vintage Raleigh motorcycles on the trailer, a Reliant Regent van. Raleigh abandoned the manufacture of motor vans in 1935, at which time Mr Williams acquired the production rights and proceeded to build the first vehicle to bear the name Reliant, at his home in Tamworth.

It is claimed that the name Reliant was chosen partly because tooling taken over from Raleigh included the provision of the letter 'R' on components, and partly because of the obvious similarity to the word 'reliable'. Unlike Raleigh who used vee-twin engines of 742 cc, Williams fitted the four-cylinder engine normally specified for the Austin Seven car. Series production commenced in about 1938, but was interrupted by war a year later.

In 1946, with the war over, production of the Reliant van re-started. The 6-cwt type accounted for most sales, but from 1950 this was joined by a slightly larger model known as the Regent. Both types were also available as open trucks. Austin had ceased manufacture of their Seven, so Reliant took over production of the engine themselves. With a compression ratio of 5.7:1, the side-valve unit was well suited to the low octane fuels then available. The Regent remained in production until about 1954, the sole survivor of the plethora of pre-war 'girder fork'-type vans, although on the final (Mark II) derivative of the Regent, this feature was concealed within a fully enclosing front body structure.

This 1952 6-cwt van, photographed at a rally in 1999, shows the primitive styling, though it has been altered slightly from the original and is now fitted with a smaller headlamp, and separate flashing direction indicators.

The first Reliant passenger car, the Regal, was announced in 1952. It used familiar mechanical components, destined to remain a Reliant feature for a further ten years. The two-seater tourer bodywork was of aluminium panelling on a hardwood frame. Where other microcars tended towards ultra-light weight with motorcycle-derived power, the Reliant Regal had far more in common with 'proper' cars, and it soon established a niche in the market place.

This restored 1953 Regal is seen being presented to the National Motor Museum in 1973. Today the car has spent well over half of its life at Beaulieu, yet seldom features in museum displays. Roger Musgrave, then marketing director at Reliant, is photographed handing the keys to a seemingly less than delighted Michael Ware, then (as now) Museum Curator.

An improved Regal followed in 1954, substantially similar to the original but with obvious alterations to the grille and the windscreen pillars and surround. Originally available only in soft-top 'Coupé' form at £403 3s 6d, the addition of a bulbous fibreglass superstructure meant that the Regal Mark II range soon included a saloon priced at an additional £10. This was followed by a van at just £353 11s 10d. All of these weighed in at less than the arbitrary 8-cwt limit at which three-wheelers ceased to be eligible for road tax at the motorcycle rate.

Realising that plastics represented the way forward in manufacturing durable cars with robust yet lightweight framework, Reliant switched over to fibreglass for the complete body of their next model, introduced in 1956 as the Regal Mark III. A further advantage was that it was possible to mould the new material to form flowing curves. The term voluptuous is perhaps not one that would spring readily to mind when describing any Reliant Regal, but certainly the cars were a mass of curves – almost potato-shaped. The specification reveals a range of features that would outclass most contemporary microcars.

Beneath the bodywork nothing had changed, but Reliant cars were becoming ever more popular. The saloon was, by now, the more usual choice, with the option of a smart two-tone colour scheme, but customers with a penchant for fresh-air motoring could still specify the coupé, which came with a folding hood in a natty contrasting colour. The brochure from which these illustrations were taken described the Regal Mark III as 'The Small Car that has everything', a claim that might have proved difficult to defend in later years of consumer protection, yet in the early 1950s to disagree would have seemed churlish.

The introduction of the Regal Mark IV in 1958 heralded a change from 6-volt to 12-volt electrical system, and with it brighter lights and therefore safer after-dark driving. Flashing direction indicators were another benefit. The horizontally sliding door windows that had hitherto been a feature were replaced by balanced-lift drop glasses. In other respects the cars were similar enough for the makers to use existing Mark III pictures to illustrate the Mark IV brochure, with but little change.

The Reliant Regal Mark V of 1960 saw some changes to the faithful chassis, albeit relatively minor ones. Wheelbase and track were both increased, the former from 74 to 75 inches, and the latter from 45 to 46 inches. The body, although of similar overall style, was substantially larger, and incorporated a squarer boot line (now accessible from outside), moulded bumpers with chromed covers, and a redesigned fascia. Oddly, the doors featured a return to horizontally sliding windows, suddenly in vogue again with the advent of the Austin 'Se7en' and Morris 'Mini-Minor' cars. Standard specification now included a second windscreen wiper, not shown in this brochure illustration.

The changes made the Regal Mark V a far more desirable car than its predecessor. The greater overall dimensions – longer and wider by 6 inches each way, and 3 inches higher – resulted in improved passenger comfort, yet it should be remembered that the Reliant remained a very small car and still conformed to the 8-cwt maximum rule, partly because of the exclusion of anything that might add more pounds avoirdupois, such as a spare wheel. The contemporary 5-cwt van was even bereft of passenger seat and bumpers.

After just one year of production the Mark V was dropped, to be replaced in 1961 by . . . the Mark VI. The recipe was much as before, but with a revised roof line giving extra headroom for rear seat passengers. Combined stop/tail and direction signal lamps were incorporated, and the instrument layout simplified. Driver visibility was improved with a deeper windscreen, and the roof rain gutters were extended. This is Mr Sixten Dalberg, a Swedish Reliant agent, with his Mark VI saloon.

Clearly Mr Average Motorist of the early 1960s was beginning to regard the side-valve Reliant as something of an anachronism, no matter what impressions the sales brochures tried to convey to the contrary. The competition was no longer the motorcycle and sidecar or the quite basic cars of the post-war decade, but the amazing Mini range, plus some exciting cars from overseas, notably Fiat's best-selling 500, the NSU Prinz, and of course the Citroën 2CV. Without some drastic changes the announcement caught on this brochure photograph could have proved somewhat prophetic. Reliant, aware of such considerations, had quietly been developing something rather special.

The all new Regal 3/25 was announced on 31 October 1962 to coincide with the Earls Court show. The up-to-the-minute styling reflected contemporary trends, while the engine was an all aluminium alloy overhead-valve unit designed and built by Reliant themselves, and one which would prove to be a grand success. The motoring press were justifiably enthusiastic, but no one seemed to notice the same old chassis lurking underneath.

Despite their apparent confidence in the new model, Reliant were hedging their bets by continuing production of the Mark VI for a few months longer. Final Mark VI models, in both saloon and commercial van forms, were equipped with the new ohv engine, creating something of a hybrid specification. This was particularly true of the van, which still harked back to earlier models in respects such as the tail lighting.

Just three days after the launch the first production 3/25, bearing the registration number 342 ENX, set off at the start of a proving run of 2,497 miles, the car being driven by Cyril 'Flash' Rogers, with his fourteen-year-old son David, and Fred Corbett. The route took the car from Birmingham Town Hall to Newcastle-upon-Tyne. There they caught the Fred Olsen line ferry *Braemar* to Oslo. Disembarking, they were met by Mr Sixten Dalberg, Swedish Reliant agent, with his Regal Mark VI. Together the two cars drove in convoy to Stockholm. The route then turned south, passing through Copenhagen, Kiel, Hamburg, Bremen and Rotterdam. A delay occurred at this point because fog had prevented the arrival of the scheduled aircraft. British United Air Ferries arranged a special flight, and their Carvair air freighter *Chelsea Bridge* brought the Reliant and its crew back to Blighty. From Southend the car was driven to Earls Court, London. Fuel consumption for the entire drive worked out at 58.1 mpg and the car performed faultlessly.

Encouraged by the success of the Scandinavian trip, Reliant loaned 342 ENX to former road-racing driver Cecil Sandford and David Cooper for the Monte Carlo Rally. The only preparation work carried out prior to the rally was a check-over at the Arthur Taylor Garage at Shipston-on-Stour, and the fitting of a sheet steel sump guard, larger diameter exhaust tailpipe, stiffer rear springs and Goodyear Ultra Grip tyres: how times have changed. Once again the car performed admirably. Of the sixty-five four-wheeled cars that started out from Glasgow, only ten arrived intact at Monte Carlo. Yet the little Reliant not only succeeded, but also made the return trip a couple of days later. Subsequently this well-travelled car also endured a trip across the Sahara Desert.

It is ten minutes to four in the final assembly shop at Tamworth. There is still plenty to do before the end of the shift, and the workforce, seemingly unaware of the photographer, are busying themselves with this mixed batch of Regal 3/25 saloons and vans. The foreman may just be seen hunched over some desk work in his office, at the far end on the right-hand side.

Besides being offered a choice of colours – blue, pale blue, signal red, pale green, white and primrose, the buyer of a new 3/25 could add such accessories to his or her new car as a spare wheel, turbo wheel trims, continental wing mirrors, ammeter, fire extinguisher, radiator grille, safety harness, or a matching high tone horn 'to give twin tone when used with the existing horn'. One major dealer, Two Strokes Limited, advertised their own version of the Regal, the TS Safari. Exactly how many TS Safari conversions were carried out is not known, but they were still being offered well into the 1970s, based on the contemporary Robin van. Other notable Two Strokes variants included the TS 'GT' Reliant saloon with high-performance engine and additional body decoration, and (later) the Bond 875 GTO.

Reliant branched out in 1964, to produce the little-known Rebel four-wheel saloon. Using mainly standard Regal components, the Rebel was regarded as overpriced and not worthy of serious consideration by most new car buyers, who went out and invested their savings in Minis and the like . . . which promptly started rusting away. Surviving Rebels of over thirty years of age often remain in good original condition. The Rebel range benefited from an engine enlargement – up from 600 to 700 cc in 1967 – and an estate car joined the saloon.

The year 1965 saw the introduction of the Regal 3/25 Super in readiness for the 1966 season. Desirable features included 'new modern front and rear styling, refined trim, a new attractive fascia, a re-positioned handbrake and enlarged door pockets'. At the same time a new range of six 'striking attractive colours' was introduced. The accountants at Reliant must have been in a generous mood, since the price of the Super was pegged at the level of the old basic model, which in turn was reduced by £18.

Eventually the basic model faded away into obscurity, and 1967 saw the arrival of the Regal DeLuxe, with features previously associated with the Super. Sales of the range continued at a satisfactory level, partly because of the low costs involved in owning and running a Reliant. The sales brochure reminds us that road tax was only £8 per year (less than half the £17 10s 0d for a four-wheeler), and that 'four people can travel in comfort from Liverpool to London on less than £1 worth of petrol'. Two months later the pound was devalued and things were never to be quite the same again.

A further development occurred in August 1968, when the 700 cc engine was fitted into the 3/25, giving a bhp rating of 31. The result was, perhaps predictably, the Regal 3/30. However, this power boost was partially negated the following year when the output was lowered by 2 of those bhp. A small fleet of 3/30 vans was operated by the Post Office as part of an exercise to examine ways of cutting costs. Previously Morris Motors had supplied most Royal Mail vans as well as those in the Post Office Telephones fleet.

The Reliant company had become highly proficient at working with fibreglass, and undertook many tasks for outside companies, among them truck cabs for the Scammell Townsman and crew-cabs for Ford's 'D' Series, generally used to modify the standard truck for vehicle recovery work. In 1967 they decided to add a medium-capacity light commercial vehicle to their own range, and this appeared as the TW9. The TW suffix was Reliant's company code for vehicles with Three Wheels, so it should be no surprise to learn that the new truck followed the general Reliant trend.

TW9 production rights were sold to BTB Engineering Ltd of Blackburn, Lancashire, towards the end of 1977. BTB were a small company, yet their twenty-five employees seem to have turned out a goodly number of Ants – the model name was only introduced after Reliant production had ceased – both trucks and derivatives. Two years into production export sales had been negotiated in Europe, Africa, the Middle East and the USA. Local authority users frequently opted for side-loading refuse collection bodies, but alternatives included fire engines, milk floats, refrigerated vans, and even some articulated wagons. The tower ladder unit could be extended to a height of 6 metres.

The Regal range continued for a few more years until its replacement, in the shape of the Reliant Robin and Super Robin, burst on to the scene in 1973. The design of the Robin was totally new, rather than just a re-style, and with its smoother and more rounded contours was right for the era. Ogle Design were responsible for the pleasing lines of the new car. Ogle had already achieved stunning results with the Bond Bug based on the same chassis, but this time their work produced a far more conservative product.

Launched with a 750 cc version of the all aluminium engine, the Robin had lively performance. When the engine was again increased in size to 850 cc, the performance was well up to modern road conditions and expectations. As this sales brochure shows, even the van was available with sporty road wheels. Not only was top speed raised, but handling improved in a manner commensurate with the increases in wheelbase and track – now 85 inches and 49 inches respectively. By now Reliant cars and vans had outgrown the microcar tag, though the company remains in business to the present day.

This delightful little car is the Lloyd 350. Unlike its Teutonic namesake, this Lloyd was made in the town of Grimsby, on the Humber estuary. Delightful though the car may be, we are not really concerned with it in this book, concentrating as we are on post-war models. However, it was this car that established Lloyd Cars Limited in 1936. The chassis, body, engine and transmission were all of what we would today call 'in-house' manufacture, and more than 250 were made before the outbreak of war intervened. The car shown was restored from discarded scrap by Jim Blezard. A mere handful of others are thought to survive world-wide.

THE

LLOYD

5-CWT.

Delivery Van.

Price - £95.

ULTRA ECONOMY

| 50 M.P.G. | 40 M.P.H. | TAX £10. |

The Lloyd 350 was of diminutive proportions, sitting on a wheelbase of just 69 inches, yet was surprisingly successful with exports to the European mainland and even South Africa. A fleet of ten was purchased by the Gas Light And Coke Company in 1938. It is not known why they didn't opt instead for the workmanlike little Lloyd van of somewhat dumpy appearance, which had a payload of 5 cwt and sold at a mere £95 in primer finish – blue or green topcoat was a further 50s.

The Lloyd with which we are really concerned here is the post-war product of the same company, the 650. First announced at the Cleethorpes Trade Fair in 1946, this car had a twin-cylinder two-stroke engine with water cooling. Once again, the makers were solely responsible for chassis, body, engine, etc.

Roland Lloyd's company were innovators, and front-wheel drive was a feature of this model and its predecessor long before the Austin/Morris Mini cars were even a twinkle in Alec Issigonis' eye. Another feature was the 'Lloyd Patented Charging Pump for delivering the fuel charge to the cylinders'. Could this have been a primitive form of fuel injection system?

The styling and build quality of the Lloyd 650 gave away nothing to products from more established car makers.

Whichever way you look at it...
A SOUND JOB

The clean symmetrical lines and handsome appearance of the LLOYD "650" will be instantly appreciated. As an open tourer it is particularly pleasing to note that the hood is completely concealed behind the rear seat squab whilst the hood and sidescreens are so designed that when erected the protection offered is equal to the average drop-head coupe. Comfort is obvious at a glance and appeal is further sharpened by almost unbelievable thrift—the result of the adaption of advanced engineering principles.

In appearance the Lloyd 650 gave away nothing to the products of far larger producers. The car was a proper four-seater, with open touring body. Weather protection comprised a substantial and well-fitting hood and rigid side screens, both of which stowed away out of sight when not in use. Independent suspension provided a comfortable ride with good handling. Like many small-scale makers, however, Lloyd Cars found they could not compete with the prices of rival models from mass-producers. The 650 was priced at £375 plus £104 18s 4d purchase tax in 1948, when £352 was the listed price for a new Ford Prefect. Lloyd Cars Limited made their last car in 1951, but the company continued trading until as late as 1983, providing specialised engineering services for some of the most prestigious of car manufacturers.

CHAPTER TWO

MOBILITY FOR A BRAVE NEW WORLD

Once it had been seen that a market existed for ultra-lightweight cars, more companies began to realise the scope for diversifying into this new field. The Festival of Britain in 1951 did much to promote forward thinking and optimism for the future – a future that would include private family motoring for the masses . . . or so the entrepreneurs hoped.

Few of the companies dipping their corporate toes into the waters of microcar production were already involved in the manufacture of vehicles, but all were willing to take a calculated gamble on their futures in the automotive arena. Hardly any would see their vehicles develop further than very limited production. This chapter is dedicated to just three of those early attempts at upward mobility.

The prototype Bond Minicar was so different from anything already in production that it is probably fair to describe it as the invention of Lawrence Bond, rather than simply a new design. Bond was an entrepreneurial enthusiast of 500 cc motor racing, and was familiar with the techniques of building ultra-lightweight vehicles. He produced a prototype, illustrated above, and with the help of his wife Pauline (shown with him in the car), managed to persuade a number of potential buyers to hand over deposits even before there were suitable premises in which to commence series production. Simple in the extreme, the ⅛-Litre Bond Shopping Car, as it was then designated, had a monocoque aluminium body and was powered by a Villiers single-cylinder engine mounted over the front wheel – features that were to remain constant to the end of Minicar production in 1966.

The styling of that original car was subsequently altered as shown, resembling more closely the Bond Minicar in its production form.

Bond's production facilities were somewhat restricted – in fact his workshop was on an upstairs level and the prototype car had been lowered down through a hatch! An agreement was finalised with Lieutenant-Colonel C.R. (Reg) Gray, Managing Director of Sharp's Commercials Ltd, to manufacture an initial batch of twenty-five Bond Minicars at their Ribbleton Lane, Preston, works. Left to right, Pauline Bond, C.P. Read (motoring journalist), Colonel Gray and Lawrence Bond celebrate the new venture.

Sharp's Commercials had a history reaching back to 1922, when motor engineer Paul Sharp started his business at Lea Garage in Preston. The garage had subsequently been bought by the Bradshaw Group of Companies and absorbed into Loxhams Garages Limited, being responsible for commercial vehicle sales and repair. More recently Sharp's had been heavily involved with the import and distribution of Chevrolet trucks under the 'Lend-Lease' scheme, and had been a major supplier of reconditioned military vehicles. As these activities were being run down in 1948 the company had ample surplus capacity, and for both parties Bond's approach was opportune indeed.

This posed 1949 photograph shows a batch of early Bonds under construction at Sharp's Commercials' workshops.

The completed car shown in the foreground of the previous photograph, and bearing the registration number CCK 919, was an early demonstrator. Here it is again, pictured on a rare original Minicar brochure. Notice the frameless windscreen of acrylic sheet: the low-powered 123 cc Villiers engine necessitated that lightweight materials were used wherever possible, and this would have had the added advantage of being less hazardous than even safety glass.

Features of the Minicar (or lack of them) included the absence of brakes for the front wheel or suspension for the rear ones. Initially steering was by a cable and bobbin system, but this was found to be unreliable (and ultimately perhaps dangerous!) so was replaced by a more conventional rack. The headlamps provided more of a glimmer than a beam, with just 6 volts and 12 watts of power. Despite frequent assertions that Bonds had to be kick-started, this was a back-up method only. The Marks A and B had a large pull-handle beneath the dashboard, with electric starting thereafter becoming the norm.

In stark contrast to the earlier photograph, which shows the factory to have been almost unbelievably clean and tidy, this view shows the same area once people had arrived and started their day's work, producing more Minicars to satisfy the increasing demand.

With almost 2,000 examples of the Bond Minicar on the road, it could be judged to have become a well-established concept. A worthy successor, tagged the Mark B, was launched on 1 July 1951. Although visually similar, the Mark B incorporated some notable improvements such as a larger more powerful Villiers engine of 197 cc, rear-wheel suspension and modifications to the rear-end design. A safety glass windscreen was by now specified as standard equipment for all Minicars. It is worth mentioning that the term Mark A was not officially recognised until the model had been replaced by the Mark B, since the longevity of the line had not previously been envisaged.

Somewhat rarer, even by Bond Minicar standards, were the Minitruck and Minivan. These were the commercial versions, and were thus sold under the Sharp's banner. The Minitruck came with an upright rear panel and larger hood for the carriage of bulky goods. Thankfully, as with most versions, this type has been saved from extinction by enthusiasts.

Rather fewer Mark B Minicars were built than Mark As, with production spanning the period June 1951 to December 1952. Shortly before the end of the period Bond introduced this delightful vehicle – the Minicar Family Safety Saloon. Obviously based upon the Minivan, it offered all-weather accommodation for the whole family, with two individual hammock seats facing each other in the back for the children. The safety element was explained by emphasising that there was no interior handle on the rear door, so the children were in no danger of falling out: a precursor of today's childproof locks!

The Coronation year of 1953 was celebrated at the Preston works of Sharp's Commercials by the announcement of the Bond Minicar Mark C. This vehicle was instantly recognisable from its precursors by virtue of the large dummy front wings, and by the provision of a small front-hinged door on the left side, though this feature was absent from the prototype. The wings, however, were not mere fashion accessories. They allowed full exploitation of the unique Bond steering linkage that allowed the whole engine/drive assembly to turn a full 180 degrees from one lock to the other, making quite spectacular manoeuvres a simple matter.

THE WORLD'S MOST ECONOMICAL CAR

A further happy consequence of the new wings was the provision of a secure location for more efficient headlamps – a real safety bonus, as was the provision of brakes on all three wheels . . . at last! Over 6,500 Mark Cs were constructed – some with fibreglass hard tops – before they were phased out in May 1956. They were very successful and provided practical transport for many, but their very usefulness was also their downfall, since they were driven literally until they fell apart, with the consequence that disproportionately few survive. This 1956 brochure shows a car bearing features that were trademarks of the later Mark D: note the grille, bumper, rear wing and decorative strips.

Not all Bonds had an easy life. This 1954 Mark C Mini-van was operated by the Sharp's Commercials factory and had covered 100,000 miles of stop-start use when it was photographed in early 1963. As the driver loads another parcel of spares for dispatch to some far-off repair-shop, we can only guess what may be contained therein. Note the trafficator in the front wing – not a common fitting.

There is a feeling among enthusiasts that the Mark D was the high point of Bond Minicar production, an opinion that would seem to be borne out by their frequent appearance at rallies. Many of the cars sold were of the family model, but a quick head-count reveals this photograph to depict a larger family than the car's makers had in mind! Despite the overcrowding – or perhaps because of it – they all seem to be having a whale of a time. At about this time a number of left-hand-drive Minicars were dispatched to North America to be sold by Craven & Hendrick Inc. of New York as the Sharp's Bearcub, but the project was not an overwhelming success. Down under, Beesley's Auto Service fared little better with the Minicars they advertised as being 'the car universally demanded throughout Australia'.

The Sharp's Commercials management felt the need to offer something of more modern appearance and this they did with the introduction of the Mark E in December 1957. Mark D and E models were produced side by side until November 1958 when both were replaced by the Mark F. This factory shot was taken in 1957 and shows Mark D models of several types. With the aid of a magnifier and the original print it is just possible to make out the shapes of two Mark E types in the distance, presumably ready for the launch of the model later that year.

The eight original prototype Mark E Minicars were actually built as early as 1956. They were of more modern full-width design, incorporating full power Lucas headlights of 7 inches diameter, proper doors on both sides, and a large luggage space at the rear, accessed by folding the seat squab forward. For the first time flashing direction indicators were fitted as standard. Sales of the Mark D were, however, so buoyant that the Mark E project was deferred. When brought out in 1957, the prototypes were found to suffer from less than satisfactory handling and by the time production cars reached the showrooms the specification had changed somewhat. The wheelbase, originally of similar proportions to the Mark D's, had been lengthened, and the rear track widened, necessitating a flaring of the rear wheel arches. Publicity brochures, printed in anticipation of an earlier launch, showed the prototype cars, easily identified by their flat rear wings. Production Mark Es were only made for a period of eleven months from December 1957, and of a total of 1,180 made, few remain unmodified.

The car shown was finished in red, but the decorative strips seem to have been added to the photograph, rather than being an original feature. The presence in the background of what appears to be a Norton motorcycle bearing the racing number 52 cannot be explained!

Opposite: 1958 also saw the opening of Britain's first section of motorway, the Preston by-pass. Sharp's Commercials achieved a useful publicity coup by arranging for a pair of their newly announced Mark F Minicars to be the first private cars to travel on the new road. A slight drawback was that in the excitement they actually drove too fast, arriving too early at the end, and missed out on a number of pre-arranged photo opportunities!

By 1958, as the end of the decade approached, Bond Minicars had enjoyed an unbroken production run of a full ten years. The Mark F model launched in November 1958 as a replacement for the short-lived Mark E proved a great success, also ousting the popular Mark D from production line and showroom alike, and was destined to take Bond into the 1960s. Yet it was, in most respects, little changed from the Mark E in its final form. For the first time, though, the engine size exceeded 197 cc – the Villiers Engineering Company were now supplying their Mark 31A power unit of 250 cc, which was good for a useful top speed of over 55 mph. Derek Revell's Mark F Tourer is seen here at a microcar rally in Germany.

The Mark F Minicar was not so much a model as a complete range, offered as Family Saloon, Ranger Van, Convertible 2-seat Tourer and Coupé – also with just two seats. Mechanically, and as regards the major body panels, all models were identical. Although considerably longer than earlier Bonds, the Mark E and F family types still offered only limited accommodation for the younger members of the family – inward facing hammock seats in what would otherwise have been regarded as the boot. This obviously meant that luggage space was restricted if all the family went out for a jaunt together. Here is a Family Saloon, performing at the Bond Owners Club Morecambe Rally.

For the carriage of goods, the Bond Mark F Ranger van was quite a useful tool, with its load area accessible through a rear hatch. Designated a commercial vehicle, it was sold at a basic price that was not subject to purchase tax, a feature that appealed to private buyers with less disposable income to play with. However, the downside was that the Ranger was considered to be in the same class as other commercial vehicles including the heaviest Fodens and Scammells, and as such shared their 30 mph maximum speed limit.

The Mark G types represented the Bond Minicar in its final form, and were made between September 1961 and September 1966, with a total production of nearly 3,250 – a huge number by microcar standards, but in modern terms a mere trifle. At launch the Mark G was available only as a saloon, in which guise it was equipped as a conventional four-seater. The body style was basically an update of the Mark F, but to bring the car into the era of the 'Swinging Sixties', and for greater headroom, the higher roof line terminated at the rear with a then-fashionable reverse-rake rear window. In many respects the Mark G could be regarded as being the grown-up version of the Minicar. It featured an altogether more advanced specification, and was intended to compete more with small conventional cars than with the microcars of yesteryear. Gone were the cable brakes – hydraulics by Girling were now standard. As a consequence the wheel size was increased from the tiny 8 inches as previously to a 10 inch diameter. The rear suspension was an all-new system of independent trailing arms with telescopic units to provide springing and damping. Much use was made of fibreglass for the body panels, and the base of the windscreen was moved forward to allow the fitting of swivelling vent windows.

Nine months into production of the Mark G Saloon, it was joined by an Estate car and similarly styled Ranger van. As before, access to the load area was via an opening rear tailgate, and the fold-down facility of the rear seats on the Estate meant that the same large payload space was available as in the Ranger.

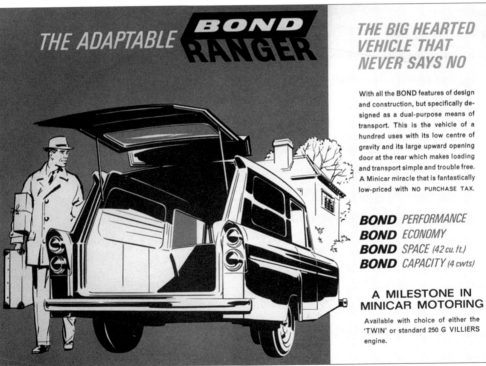

THE ADAPTABLE **BOND RANGER**

THE BIG HEARTED VEHICLE THAT NEVER SAYS NO

With all the BOND features of design and construction, but specifically designed as a dual-purpose means of transport. This is the vehicle of a hundred uses with its low centre of gravity and its large upward opening door at the rear which makes loading and transport simple and trouble free. A Minicar miracle that is fantastically low-priced with NO PURCHASE TAX.

BOND PERFORMANCE
BOND ECONOMY
BOND SPACE (42 cu. ft.)
BOND CAPACITY (4 cwts)

A MILESTONE IN MINICAR MOTORING

Available with choice of either the 'TWIN' or standard 250 G VILLIERS engine.

By 1963 sales of all microcars were in sharp decline. In an attempt to prolong the market-life of the Minicar range Bond offered the option of a twin-cylinder Villiers 4T engine (still a two-stroke, and still with a total displacement of only 250 cc) from March 1963. Eagerly seized upon by faithful Bond buyers who desired smoother mechanical running, the twin later came to be regarded as less satisfactory than the traditional single-cylinder type.

Despite the more sophisticated specification and the introduction of the 250 Twin option, the line on sales graphs maintained its downward path. Clearly it was time for the future of the Minicar range to be given careful consideration. Realising that the market was changing and that the era of the microcar was coming to an end, the decision was taken to diversify into other areas. This diversification took the form of the Bond Equipe GT, a stylish 'fast-back' coupé based on the Triumph Herald chassis, floor, scuttle and mechanical units. The lines of the Equipe were styled to accommodate the Herald doors, and the car was individualistic yet practical – with service and parts availability as with the regular Triumph product.

The Minicar still had one more trick up its sleeve, though, and this was revealed with the launch of the Mark G Tourer in 1964. The Tourer lacked some of the decoration of others in the Mark G range; the vent windows did not open, there were no chromed strips on the wings, and the twin engine was available only to special order. But at a time when some of the larger manufacturers were offering the option of fresh-air motoring with convertibles based on the Hillman Minx and Super Minx, Triumph Herald and Morris Minor, anything was worth trying.

The Equipe proved an instant success, with sales restricted more by the slow pace of construction than by any lack of market appeal. It might have been expected that the makers would divert entirely to this new venture, yet they were well aware that to place their dependence upon vital supplies from a single source, not to mention relying too much on the whims of an untried section of the buying public, would be foolhardy. There were many thousands of faithful Bond customers for whom the Equipe was merely an anachronism. They expected Bonds to have three wheels. Bond Cars, as the company had re-christened itself, did not fail its customers.

In August 1965, while the Mark G was still being made, Bond astonished the world with the introduction of the 875, a totally new projectile that could hurtle along at over 90 mph, thanks to the 875 cc four-cylinder Hillman Imp power unit installed at the rear and Bond's lightweight fibreglass and alloy bodywork. Clearly, as was shown by 'Bond Bird' Irene Bassey in 1967, Bond buyers had come a long way since the photograph was taken of the family in the Mark C!

The 875 had actually spent some time in the development stage. This 1965-registered pre-production car, seen with racing driver John Surtees, displays an uncluttered appearance. Production cars incorporated styling mouldings at the front and on the bonnet, but lost the hinged rear windows and bright bumper trims. Surtees was testing the car at Brands Hatch, where he attained speeds over 100 mph and set an unofficial lap record!

Bonds of various types were made alongside each other for a time. This shot shows Mark G types being made ready for delivery, with an 875 displaying 'show' number plates beyond. To the left is a line of GT4S Equipes, the model that replaced the GT in 1964. The date is presumed to be 1965.

The labour force responsible for making the fibreglass bodywork was largely female. This was before the wearing of jeans or trousers became commonplace, and the lack of adequate protective clothing would not be tolerated in later years. It cannot have been a comfortable environment in which to work, but everyone appears to be quite happy.

More happy workers. The front section of the 875 was made separately, as can be seen here. In front of the 875 bodyshell newly released from its mould is one for an Equipe GT4S, in a similar condition. On the far side of the workshop, the girl in the dark overall seems to have her tea cup right next to her mixing bowl! There were no COSHH regulations in the workplace in those swinging '60s days.

A commercial version of the Bond 875 was part of the package, and carried on the traditional Ranger model name. This was similar to the saloon but the rear side windows were not cut out. At the back an opening hatch was incorporated for loading. With the potential for 90 mph performance many owners must have been tempted to flout the 30 mph limit imposed on the Ranger because of its commercial vehicle status.

From March 1968 the 875 saloon underwent a facelift to become the Mark 2, the last real Bond car. While retaining most of the original features, the second-generation model had a re-styled nose with fashionable rectangular headlamps. At the same time the bonnet aperture was very much enlarged, and an aluminium grille fitted. Within the cabin the colour was changed from grey to black and the seating was improved. In this form the 875 continued in production until February 1970. The Ranger van did not receive the styling update. Whether or not the 875 was such a beauty is a matter for the beholder. We can only wonder at what might have followed had history taken a different course.

The shock news of 1969 was that Bond Cars Ltd had been bought out by their arch rivals, the Reliant Motor Company, and that production at Preston would be run down and the site closed. In effect, Reliant had in one fell swoop removed their major competitor, both in the field of three-wheeler production and that of sports saloons – Bond's Equipe, by now powered by the Triumph Vitesse six-cylinder engine, competed for the same market as Reliant's Scimitar – and had bought the rights to use the Bond name with its established and loyal customer base. To soften the blow, Reliant announced that their new model, a sporting three-wheeler unlike anything seen before, would carry the Bond name.

The Bond Bug was a wedge-shaped fibreglass car that resembled no other. Using standard Reliant components, its sporting image was to appeal to the youthful and trendy buyers for whom the staid Regal three-wheelers were anathema. It was available only in orange, and there were three levels of trim.

The Bond Bug was launched at a high profile ceremony at Woburn on 7 June 1970. Pre-launch production had commenced in March, and these original cars were, in fact, built at Preston before going to Tamworth for finishing. By May 114 cars had been completed, including the one and only example of the basic version, and some 500 cars were said to be in the showrooms by early August, with plans to step up production to fifty units per week.

The caption on the reverse of this press photo reads: 'A consignment of Bugs leaving Two Gates for Woburn Abbey Press Conference', though interestingly the same picture was used in *Reliant Review* of August 1970 to show 'transporters carrying Bugs to destinations all over the country'. Notice the unregistered Reliant Regal vans in the background.

The revolutionary design of the Bond Bug was the work of the Ogle Design studio. Here, Tom Karen, Managing Director of Ogle, is seen standing at the back of a Bug while R.W. Wiggin, Reliant's MD, sits down for a BBC interview at the launch.

Reliant Motors pulled out all the stops to promote the Bug, which was described as the 'youth car of the '70s'. Bugs were photographed with celebrities including comedians Bob Monkhouse and (as seen here) a youthful Jimmy Tarbuck; Bugs were loaned to the *Daily Sketch* newspaper for the use of their 'Guinea Girls'; Bugs were shown on the Blue Peter and Wheelbase television programmes; and one Bug was featured as the star prize on the popular *Golden Shot* television game show. Historical note: the *Daily Sketch* instigated a promotion at seaside resorts around the country. 'Guineas Girls' handed out rewards to the value of one guinea (21s) to anyone seen carrying a current copy of the paper.

The London Motor Show took place in the autumn of 1970, just when the initial rush of 'Bugmania' could have been expected to show signs of wearing thin. Officially only four-wheeled cars were eligible for inclusion, but this ruling only served to provide yet another publicity opportunity for the men at Tamworth, who built a special back-to-back Bug with four wheels as shown. It is said that enquiries were met with the statement that the company would not sell the show car, but could supply half of it. The car is shown here baffling the residents of Scarborough in 1971.

Production Bond Bugs were to have been sold in three versions; Bug 700, without side screens or other refinements; Bug 700E, with sidescreens, heater, telescopic canopy damper, driver's-side sun visor and interior light; Bug 700ES, as above plus higher-compression engine, alloy wheels (including a spare on this model only), low profile tyres, wing mirrors, mud flaps, 'Formula 1' steering wheel, etc. In the event only one Bug 700 was built, with a combined total of 2125 700E and ES models. From October 1973 the engines were increased to 750 cc, and the model designations changed accordingly, although only 142 such cars were made.

Reliant Motors called the standard colour for all Bugs Tangerine. A very small number were painted in other colours for promotional use. Rothman's specified a white livery, and Roses requested green to publicise their Lime Juice Cordial. The Cape fruit promotional car shown here is in white and appeared in a series of television commercials. Immortality was thrust upon the Bug when it was made in model form by Corgi as part of their 'Whizzwheels' series, but for the full-size version the end came in May 1974 when the Reliant Motor Company deleted the model, and with it the Bond name.

The Russon car was the brain-child of Mr D.A. Russell, who became something of an entrepreneur following the Second World War. Among his other business interests were publishing and models. He was able to combine the two in the magazine *Aeromodeller*, of which he was Managing Editor. In 1946 the old aerodrome at Eaton Bray, near Leighton Buzzard, was purchased, and work commenced on buildings to house the *Aeromodeller* offices. In due course it was the Eaton Bray premises that were to see development of the Russon car.

Russon Cars Ltd was incorporated on 18 January 1950. The first prototype Russon was constructed mainly to test the chassis and 197 cc Villiers engine prior to building a production-style body. In this form the car covered many miles around the Chiltern hills, with at least one trip to London. The aluminium body, never intended as more than a prototype, was left unpainted. The driver here is designer Derek Currie; passengers are Timothy (centre) and Michael Russell. A ride in the car was one of the few privileges of being the boss's son! Notice the external speedometer below the mirror. The car bears its correct 1950 Bedfordshire registration, which was retained for further developments.

As a result of the trials a second chassis was designed, incorporating modified suspension and engine-mounting arrangements. Russon employed a female member of staff – Gabrielle Elwell, wife of the Works Manager – to weld up the chassis/frames. At the same time a small team of skilled workers was assembled and some of these transformed the Russon to the second prototype version, seen here. The bodywork was of aluminium panels, hand beaten by ex-Cooper panel-beater Ivan Miles, on an ash frame built by Alf Palmer.

In this form the now very attractively styled Russon, with a front end treatment remarkably similar to that utilised by the makers of the Triumph TR2 and TR2 sports cars, and finished in light blue, covered many more miles on test. Already, at this prototype stage, the Russon is possibly the prettiest of microcars, certainly of its day, though it might have been better to wait for the summer weather before taking the photographs!

With the stylish new body and upgraded chassis, the power of the 197 cc engine was found to be insufficient. The answer was to invest in a larger power unit, and the type selected was the Excelsior 'Talisman Twin' 250, which being a twin-cylinder type had the advantage of providing smoother running. At the same time the chassis underwent a few more minor changes, and there was yet another prototype body.

This view shows the final development of the Russon chassis, with a group of proud company employees. Derek Currie is on the extreme left of the picture, and Michael Russell is at the opposite end of the group. The absence of D.A. Russell himself suggests that he might have been the photographer.

On Russon number three the front grille was dispensed with (the engine was at the rear anyway), and the wing line continued as a flowing curve right through to the back. The windscreen acquired a frame, but not wipers. A space was created behind the seats for stowage of the hood, and carriage of luggage.

This car was used as the basis for publicity brochures, as shown, although there had been a previous brochure, showing the second prototype Russon modified with air-brush artwork to resemble the later model. This third car was finished in dark red. The Russon badge displayed so prominently was designed by Michael Russell, and betrays quite considerable pride in the car.

Thorough road testing took place throughout the spring of 1951, with delivery of completed cars promised for July of that year. Between publication of the brochure and production of the cars, and with the warmer spring days, it was found that the air-cooled engine had a tendency to run hot in its sheltered environment in what would normally be considered the boot. To overcome this problem the front grille was re-instated, with ducted air passing below the passenger compartment. Extractor grilles were also provided above the engine.

Production of the Russon, now in its final form, began in earnest. The figure seen towards the left, arc-welding the next chassis, is presumed to be Mrs Elwell, nicknamed 'the Angel Gabriel' in recognition of her skills with the welding torch. It is not known whether these shop-floor pictures were specially posed, but the floor in the assembly shop looks suspiciously clean!

D.A. Russell himself, accompanied by his wife as navigator, drove the first 'production type Russon car' presumably the final prototype (still registered HMJ 263) on a 1,525-mile tour visiting dealers throughout the southern half of England and Wales between 28 July and 11 August 1951. On arrival at each of the appointed garages the car was made available for demonstration runs. The sequence of venues was departure from Stanbridge to Wembley, Northampton, Ipswich, Gerrards Cross and home to Boxmoor, then to Cheltenham, Bournemouth and Bedford, and home to Boxmoor again, then Chatham and Abergavenny, finally returning to Stanbridge. The car behaved impeccably throughout, with an adjustment to the brakes being the only attention needed, and no involuntary stops.

Only six or seven genuine production cars are recalled as having been delivered to customers before the company failed late in 1951. A further two or three cars may be added to this total, but no firm evidence exists. The number three prototype, suitably upgraded, became the last Russon car to be sold. The car shown here with trade plates was apparently ready for delivery, and the justification for the photograph may have been that it was the first such, delivered to a dealer in London as a demonstrator, then sale car.

Eventually the assets of the Russon company were disposed of by the Official Receiver. Much, including materials and tools – even a pile of scrap aluminium offcuts – was purchased by Air Vice Marshal D.C.T. Bennett, in preparation for starting work on a project of his own – the Fairthorpe Atom. The company was eventually dissolved in 1957.

Shown here is the only known photograph of a Russon in later life. This car bears a Bath registration, possibly indicating that it was sold by the Cheltenham dealer, Walker & Ward Limited, and is no longer in the pristine state in which it would have left Eaton Bray. The presence of the model aircraft is a remarkable coincidence, bearing in mind the early history of the company. Sadly no examples of the Russon car seem to have survived.

The angular Rodley was made for a few months in 1954 and 1955 at Airedale Mills, in the suburb of Leeds from which it took its name. Owing little to the design of any other car, it was a steel-bodied saloon designed by one Henry Brown. With its four wheels and 750 cc engine size (JAP twin cylinder) it should really be excluded from the pages of this book, but the intentions of its maker were probably broadly in line with many of its slightly smaller competitors so to exclude it on grounds of mere size would seem churlish.

The story goes that the Rodley was selected to spearhead a campaign by the Co-operative movement to sell new cars through Co-operative furniture outlets. This led to disputes with suppliers of component parts, notably the Lucas electrical group and the Dunlop tyre company. The consequent component shortages meant that few Rodley cars were built.

This publicity shot shows an early car equipped with Lucas lights, but the tyres appear to be of Michelin pattern, on three-stud (Renault?) wheels. Note the sunshine roof – standard equipment on many cars in those days – and the simple door handles. Flashes of the gentleman driver's trouser braces would have been quite unremarkable in 1954, even in a promotional photograph.

Despite its apparently small dimensions, the Rodley was a full four-seater, the front seat tipping forward to allow the lady in her 1950s flowery dress access to the back.

Around sixty-five Rodley cars are reported to have found buyers. Most, if not all, were beset by the sort of problems that might have been ironed out during the course of a longer period of production. When running, the engine caused the whole car to vibrate violently – a problem that could probably have been rectified quite simply with modified engine mountings – but perhaps more serious was a most unfortunate propensity for the car to self-combust because of the proximity of sound-proofing material to the hot exhaust pipe. This factor did little to help the survival rate of the cars, and the last known survivor sadly met its doom in a scrapyard at the age of about thirty years, nobody having considered it worth saving.

Mr Brown was not put off by the difficulties encountered, though, and went on to design the rather more successful Scootacar, built a few miles away in Hunslet.

CHAPTER THREE

HIGH HOPES BUT SECOND DIVISION RESULTS

As the 1950s continued, so companies already involved with other aspects of industry joined the growing throng of microcar makers. This chapter spotlights the attempts of three such companies: Bonallack & Son, the Electrical Engineering and Construction Company, and S.E. Opperman Ltd. All had sound engineering experience and expertise behind them. Each approached the design and manufacture of microcars in their own way, but ultimately none lasted more than a few seasons in the increasingly competitive world of microcars.

Almost unknown outside the realms of the true microcar enthusiast, the EEC Co. Workers' Playtime of 1952, which took its name from the popular BBC wireless programme of the time, is the only make of car known to have emanated from the small Devon coastal town of Totnes. The manufacturing company was the Electrical Engineering and Construction Company Ltd. This company, previously known by the name Curtis Engineering, built Royal Navy minesweepers during the Second World War. A.J. Stubbings, who had dealt with the running of the company, took over with a partner, and began making various items including generator equipment for early jet aircraft.

Sadly, little is known of the immediate background to the car, but people involved with the project have stated that just one example was produced, this being shown in publicity shots with the 'false' pre-war Cornish registration number FAF 227. The design, somewhat radical for the period, was by Richard 'Dick' Turpin and a Mr Miller. Reg Bowhay led a team of three who translated the drawings into a car of single curvature alloy panels on an electrically welded steel frame, the most startling innovation being the use of a single opening front section to the car, rather like that claimed to be so revolutionary when the Isetta was announced in Italy in 1953. This feature was made possible by locating the engine, a 250 cc Excelsior two-stroke twin, at the back, where it drove the single rear wheel. The car was finished in grey and blue.

One of the least known of the multitude of British-built microcars is the delightfully named Minnow. First announced as early as 1951, the Minnow was a product of commercial vehicle bodybuilders Bonallack & Son, who occupied premises at Forest Gate in East London. In this early view it is just possible to make out details of an AEC Monarch truck in the background, which appears to have been fitted with a tanker body by the Bonallack company. Further into the background can be seen the radiator grille of a Bedford 'O' Type truck, probably the most common type on the roads of the time. With their normal line of work apparently so plentiful, one wonders why Bonallack bothered with the Minnow at all.

A brand new Minnow, possibly the company demonstrator, dwarfed by the AEC lorry. With its air scoops on the sides and all the ventilation louvres on top and at the rear, the Minnow should not have been troubled by overheating or fuel vapourisation. The interior seems quite civilised, with dash-mounted cubby-hole and oval instrument panel typical of the period.

Sadly very few Minnows found purchasers. Perhaps it was the lack of dealer facilities, or perhaps the price of £468 – at a time when a '1937 model MG 2-litre drop-head coupé, made practically new car at Abingdon 1946' was advertised in Autocar for only £400 – had something to do with it. Nevertheless the Minnow probably seemed luxurious to the Bonallack employees who arrived at work on the bicycles in the background. The panel leaning against the side of the car has been removed from the tail to allow access to the engine.

Later production Minnows differed from the original in that there was an opening lid at the front, perhaps intended for a small amount of luggage to be stowed within. There were no exterior door handles; opening the doors from outside when the weather protection was in place involved lifting the flap provided below the side window, though its primary function was to enable the driver to give hand signals. The engine was a 250 cc Excelsior two-stroke twin – a popular choice for microcars in the early to mid-1950s.

S.E. Opperman Ltd was a company with roots going back to 1860, when Mr C.D. Opperman set up as a wheel cutter and engineer in Clerkenwell, London. The company developed under a succession of directors, gradually moving into the field of gear-making for automotive and early aeronautical applications, though still continuing in other spheres.

In 1940 Opperman moved to a purpose-built factory at Stirling Corner, Boreham Wood, and in 1947 the Opperman Motocart was announced. These vehicles were rarely seen on the roads, being intended for farm, factory and council use. Familiarity will mainly have been achieved through the Dinky Toys model, faithfully reproduced in miniature and sold from 1949 to 1961. Whether the Motocart itself conforms to the general specification expected of a microcar is open to question, but certainly the single-cylinder (JAP) engine and three-wheel configuration tend to suggest it does. The Motocart proved very successful in terms of sales and longevity, and some are still at work fifty years on, with others awaiting the restorative attentions of enthusiasts.

With a wide range of products adorning the company history, including racecourse totalisator equipment, coal-washing plant, conversions to old BBC-only television sets to enable them to receive the then new ITV programmes, the design for the Admiralty's first welded-construction midget submarines, and a 'hidden' zip fastener, it was probably not a surprise that Opperman should eventually dabble in microcars. This dabble initially took the form of the Unicar, claimed elsewhere to have been designed by none other than Lawrence Bond, of Minicar fame. Seen here in surroundings that might have been better suited to an Armstrong Siddeley is an early Unicar demonstrator, actually the work of designer George Trolley, whom Norman Gillard, Opperman's Quality Manager, remembers as 'the fastest man I have ever seen with a pencil'.

The Unicar came on to the market in 1956, initially powered by a rear-mounted British Anzani engine of 322 cc, giving a claimed 15 bhp, and 55 mpg. Later versions boasted an increased power output of 18 bhp, which was achieved by fitting the 328 cc Excelsior engine as standard, with a claimed 75 mpg. Note also that the windscreen wiper was moved from the top to the bottom of the screen and acquired a twin for the passenger's side, and the apparent restyle of the rear wing and deletion of the separate sill moulding.

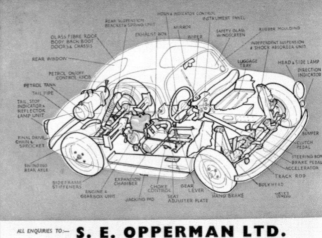
The Unicar was the cheapest car exhibited at the 1956 London Motor Show, but with its four-wheel configuration was subject to a higher cost road fund licence than contemporary three wheelers. A few examples were sold in kit form, which reduced the price still further, and avoided the need for purchase tax to be charged. Accommodation was fairly spartan, yet reasonably comfortable, with hammock-style front seats and child seats in the rear, either side of an access hatch to the engine. A luggage boot was not a feature. Notable, though, was the parcel shelf, which was sufficiently commodious to swallow up the 12 inch spare wheel and probably a week's shopping as well!

Opperman made the bold move of unveiling their all new coupé, the Stirling (the name reflected their address but had useful motor racing connotations as well), at the London Motor Show of 1958. The car displayed was a vast improvement on the old Unicar, with a stylish coupé body – again the work of George Trolley – that looked just right. To achieve this result, a full-sized Plaster of Paris model had first been constructed (below), from which the body moulds (one each of top and bottom, to be joined at the 'swage' line half way up) were made. Apparently one of the first comments received came from a certain Mr Moss, who telephoned to object to the unauthorised use of his name.

Two prototypes of the Stirling were made before the decision was taken not to proceed with the project, allegedly because of difficulties in obtaining components owing to the impending launch of the Austin/Morris Mini models. The Stirling was said to have created rather too much interest, with the result that certain essential components suddenly became 'not available'. Sadly the Motor Show car, registered as 694 DRO, was subsequently loaded on to a council lorry and taken away to the dump. It is fortunate that the cameras were clicking first before this took place.

The Excelsior twin power unit fitted to 694 DRO was unusual in that it was bored out to give a capacity of 424 cc, with the increased performance that would be expected of what would later have been termed a 'GT' car. The sales brochures prepared for the launch list no alternative engine for the Stirling, so we have to assume it would have remained thus, except . . .

. . . the second prototype was almost identical in terms of design, but a new 500 cc power plant from the Austrian Steyr Puch company was fitted, incorporating gearbox and transaxle. This engine being equipped with a fuel pump, the tank was moved to share the front compartment with the spare wheel, and the filler cap was tucked away out of sight. In left-hand-drive form the car successfully covered many kilometres proving itself around Europe. So successfully, in fact, that the eventual intention was to supply the cars without engines direct to Steyr Puch, for completion and direct sale throughout Europe. However, this was not to be. 487 FRO was among the company assets to be sold when Opperman ceased trading in 1959. It was tracked down in 1979 (above) and is now secure in preservation – a reminder of what could have provided very real competition for the BMC Mini.

CHAPTER FOUR

THE DESIGNS OF DAVID GOTTLIEB

David Gottlieb, along with Lawrence Bond, was one of the most prolific designers of British microcars, and was responsible for some of the more stylish creations that come into the sphere of this book. He is known to have been the force behind the drawing board for three vehicles, each of which demonstrates Gottlieb's flair for long flowing curves, starting with the much maligned Allard Clipper, then the Powerdrive and the Coronet. Three cars that failed to capture the mass market, for reasons other than mere design shortcomings, but which suggest a vision for design and style that was far in advance of its time.

Two of Gottlieb's creations utilised the new fibreglass material, while the third was clad in lightweight aluminium. Chassis designs were original in every case, though to reduce costs there was a willingness to incorporate many bought-in components. None of Gottlieb's designs became a best-seller, but in hindsight we are left wondering if that was in spite of his work, rather than because of it.

Sidney Allard first became involved with the making of cars to his own specification in 1937 at Adlards Motors Ltd, Putney, South London. In 1946 he branched out to form Allard Motor Co. Ltd, not far away at Clapham, leaving Adlards to continue as Ford dealers. The Allard company built cars with an eye to the performance market, using high-powered engines, usually from American manufacturers. In 1952 Sidney Allard won the Monte Carlo Rally in one of his own P Type saloons.

The following year David Gottlieb's Powerdrive company was looking for someone to take on the manufacture of their newly designed three-wheeled car. Following an introduction via a Mr Michael Christie in 1953, in recognition of which Mr Christie was to receive a commission payment of 10s per car sold, an agreement was negotiated. The result was the car that became the Allard Clipper.

Proud owners – well-known London motor dealer Raymond Way with his wife and their 'his and hers' Allards – P1 and Clipper.

Once the project had been accepted by Allard, a separate company, the Allard Clipper Company Ltd, was formed. Gilbert Jepson, an engineer of some years' experience, was given the task of constructing a prototype chassis, and this was quickly accomplished, incorporating the use of such readily available components as BSA A7 motorcycle steering head races, a Burman Steering box as fitted to the Ford 8, and Morris Minor brake assemblies. A Villiers 346 cc single-cylinder engine was fitted ahead of the left-hand rear wheel, which it drove via a Burman gearbox. Mr Jepson recalls having to modify the original design to maintain the geometry of the driven

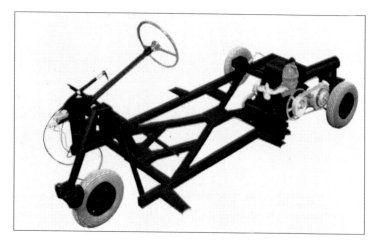

wheel under power, but in most respects the Gottlieb design, actually flowing from the pen of a Mr Tungey, was adhered to. The Hordern-Richmond company of Haddenham was commissioned to produce bodywork from the then innovative fibreglass material.

The first bodyshell was received from Haddenham on 19 March 1954, with a time span from conception to reality that would be incomprehensible to later generations of motor manufacturers. Less than one month later, on 15 April, the completed car had been registered and licensed, and already showed an odometer reading of 517 miles. The next day (Good Friday) Mr Jepson undertook a return trip from South London to Matlock, which was trouble free apart from the failure of the tyre on the driven wheel. OXX 552 was retained by Allard as a 'works car', and used as a test-bed for such alternative power units as a JAP side-valve engine, and a British Anzani twin-cylinder two-stroke.

Motor dealer Raymond Way had large premises in Kilburn and at Seven Kings, and was keen to be involved as a Clipper dealer. This as-yet unregistered example seems to have suffered a minor scrape to its front corner. Behind it a large car of American origin shows signs of a hard time as it finishes its days as a stock car. The depressing surroundings are typical of inner-city environments in the decade following the end of the war, and gaily coloured cars such as the Clipper (this one would have been ivory, but others had the main body finished in red or pale blue) did much to lighten the scene.

The interior of the Allard Clipper was uncomplicated to the point of austerity. In the centre of the fascia can be seen (left to right) the combined ignition and lighting switch, the speedometer and the starter button. Other controls not visible in this view include the horn push, windscreen wiper switch and headlamp dipper. The bench seat is covered in 'Vynide'. There are no side windows, but clear flexible side curtains could be attached for wet weather use.

Small children never change. These two young misses, members of the post-war 'baby-boom', demonstrate the fresh-air pleasures of riding in the dickey seat, an optional extra left over from a bygone age that seems not to have been specified by any original Allard Clipper buyers. Matching the scrape at the front of the car can be seen the tell-tale marks of petrol-oil mix running down from the fuel filler cap atop the rear wing.

The total absence of any form of direction indicators necessitates the driver having plenty of space to give adequate hand signals. It is easy to forget how many of the facilities we take for granted in the modern car are relatively late additions, yet how advanced a car like the Clipper would have seemed to someone more accustomed to a (probably) pre-war side-valve-engined motorcycle and sidecar combination for family transport.

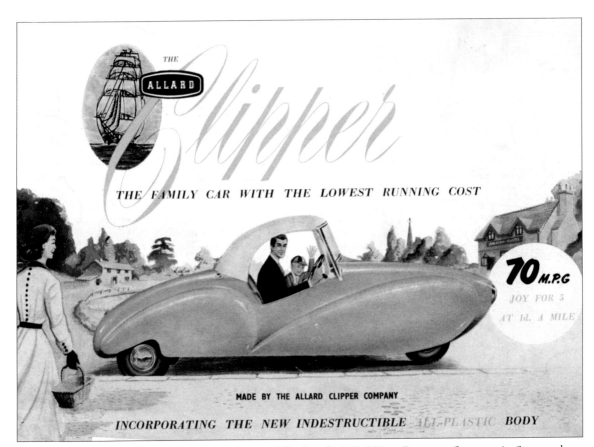

THE
ALLARD *Clipper*

THE FAMILY CAR WITH THE LOWEST RUNNING COST

70 M.P.G
JOY FOR 5
AT 1d. A MILE

MADE BY THE ALLARD CLIPPER COMPANY

INCORPORATING THE NEW INDESTRUCTIBLE ALL-PLASTIC BODY

In order to evaluate and compare the competition, Allard took OXX 552 to Ranmore Common in Surrey, along with an AC Petite and a Bond Minicar. Regrettably no records of putting the cars through their paces seem to have survived. However, a trip undertaken by two Clippers on 22 February 1955 to Bingley Hall, Birmingham, for the purpose of showing the cars on BBC television has been noted. Sidney Allard created considerable excitement by driving one of the pair on two wheels, though whether this was intentional or just the result of some over-exuberant manoeuvring is not known.

Far removed from the earlier shots of inner-city streets, this delightful artist's impression shows the Allard Clipper as illustrated on the original sales brochure. Brightly printed in full colour, it suggests a 'Cinemascope' image of the car. One can only hope that buyers were not too disappointed with the real thing.

By the early part of 1955 it had become apparent that Hordern-Richmond's costings for the manufacture of the Clipper body were inaccurate, and there were requests from them for a not inconsiderable increase in the price. This would have necessitated an overall rise in the selling price that was deemed unacceptable. At the same time other difficulties were occurring. Bodies were made individually at Haddenham and then collected in Allard's Ford van, and the non-arrival of an expected body on 24 June 1955 brought production to an impromptu halt, which would have hastened the demise of the project. The initial production run of one hundred units was aborted after only about twenty-two cars had been completed, bringing to an acrimonious end both the Allard Clipper project and the association between David Gottlieb's Powerdrive company and Allard. Just two Allard Clippers are known to survive, one of them, chassis number CA 131, in a museum in Germany. 906 CMT, chassis CA 111, is the sole example in England. Thus examples of what one writer has unkindly described as 'one of the ugliest British bubble cars' from both ends of the production run are still extant.

With the Allard Clipper project abandoned in 1955, David Gottlieb set about designing a successor. This car, totally different in the manner and material of construction, the wheel configuration and choice of power unit, was made at Wood Green, London, and sold under the Powerdrive company's own name, with the Blue Star Garages chain appointed distributors for the United Kingdom. A full-width convertible body of aluminium panelling offered up-to-the-minute styling and accommodation for three abreast on the bench seat, but the lion's head badge looked suspiciously like somebody's front door knocker.

The front 'bonnet' actually concealed one of the luggage compartments. With suspension borrowed from a manufacturer of more conventional cars, there was less space beneath than might have been expected. The remaining luggage space was alongside the 322 cc British Anzani engine at the rear of the car. Despite being nearly 12 feet long, 4 feet 7 inches wide, and 4 feet 4 inches high, the weight was under 8 cwt, and a top speed of 60 mph and fuel consumption of 65 mpg were claimed, but such claims were not easy to substantiate.

The Powerdrive was listed from 1956 to 1958, but relatively few were sold at the list price of £412, when a Reliant Regal with four seats and a proper four-cylinder engine could be bought new for £8 less. Today a Powerdrive in this condition would command a high price – as would any of the cars in the background. The sad fact is that with the high scrap value of the aluminium bodywork probably none has survived in a condition that could be described other than as having potential for restoration.

The Coronet made its first public appearance in June 1957. Another of David Gottlieb's designs, it was marketed by Coronet Cars Ltd of Denham, Bucks. The premises exist today as a Texaco petrol station. In 1957 it was a branch of the Blue Star Garage chain, and production of the Coronet initially took place in a building at the rear. By the end of the year manufacture had been transferred to James Whitson & Company, of West Drayton (Whitson was a contraction of Whittit & Son), already well established in the field of commercial and passenger vehicle manufacture, on behalf of Blue Star Garages, who remained sponsors and distributors.

Previous Whitson projects had included panel work for the prototypes of London Transport's Routemaster bus, some unorthodox rear-engined Foden coaches, almost the entire fleet of 'Green Goddess' fire engines, and the then revolutionary observation body for the Maudslay coach, a faithfully reproduced Dinky Toys model of which was sold from 1950 to 1960. More recently Whitson's produced bodywork for Peerless and Warwick cars, Winchester taxicabs, and the Slough-assembled Citroën Bijou cars. The Bijou (illustrated) was developed by the British arm of Citroën as an anglicised version of the 2CV, and now attracts a cult following in its own right.

Chassis fabrication and production of the glassfibre reinforced bodywork for the Coronet proceeded simultaneously at West Drayton. It can be seen that the chassis were very solidly made. This view shows completed chassis units, fronts facing the camera. One wonders whether the wearing of head gear was a tradition at Whitson's, or if it was just a cold place to work. The collar and tie suggest a position of authority in the workshop.

Body production was carried out in a controlled temperature of between 70 and 80 degrees Fahrenheit, with about six hours' setting time. When the body sections were fully cured, they were mated to the chassis. Excelsior power units were bought in ready to fit, as were suspension and steering components, thought to be derived from the Standard 8 car.

With lights and interior installed, the hood is fitted. In this picture it is evident that the front wheels are still covered over to protect them from overspray when the car was painted. Unusually for a fibreglass-bodied car, the Coronet did not have a pigmented gel-coat, instead receiving one coat of primer filler, followed by two coats of spray enamel.

The Coronet was marketed as a full three-seater, and as this view shows this seems to be a fully justifiable claim. Regrettably few pictures show the car with its hood and side screens closed, but perhaps this is just as well as the cleanly flowing lines were not enhanced when the weather protection was in use.

Seen in the grounds of James Whitson's West Drayton factory, the very attractive Coronet and its equally pretty driver post for the camera in 1957. Total production of Coronet cars, which were catalogued from 1957 to 1960, is believed to have been between 250 and 500. Few have survived into preservation. One hopes the lady model (and her hat) have fared better.

CHAPTER FIVE

AUSTRIA'S OWN MICROCAR: THE FELBER

The Felber Autoroller was one of that rare breed of cars built in Austria. A. Felber & Co. was already the largest builder of motorcycle sidecars in Austria, and the microcar venture could be seen as a logical progression to exploit the mood of the day, when so many buyers were being weaned off motorcycles and into cars. Between 380 and 400 examples were built in 1953 and 1954 in a country not renowned for its industrial prowess.

The company's links with microcars did not end with the abandonment of the Autoroller, but turned to the distribution and selling of Victoria, Spatz, Heinkel and Trojan products. Production facilities were switched to the manufacture of industrial washing machines.

Few Felbers survive to this day, perhaps because of their owners' enthusiasm for competing in the Bergrennen uphill races rather than any faults with the cars.

The world was first made aware of the Felber in 1952, when an Austrian motoring journalist writing under the pseudonym Christmann announced that series production was about to commence. The vehicle illustrated here was, in fact, the penultimate of several prototypes: it was of unusual design, and was powered by a rear-mounted Rotax twin-cylinder two-stroke engine of 350 cc, driving through a four-speed gearbox. Only a single headlamp was fitted, and a single windscreen wiper, for the portion of windscreen ahead of the driver. The Frau is evidently enjoying a trip out with her family.

By the time series production had commenced in 1953 the Felber had grown up, as this sales brochure illustrates, and had been designated the T 400 model. The more elaborate bodywork offered rather better protection from the elements, there were now two headlamps (but still just one wiper), and to cope with the extra weight and wind resistance the engine size had increased to 398 cc. Compare the apparent dimensions of the car in this artist's impression with those of the following photographs.

The simple chassis provided a tubular steel perimeter with flat floor, and a tubular hoop at the front end. This illustration shows how the controls were offset to the left – Felbers were never right-hand drive. The seating accommodation remained unorthodox throughout, with the primary passenger seat behind the driver and offset to the right, and an occasional/child seat on the left, behind the driver. Each front wheel had an ingenious suspension arrangement using separate coil springs and telescopic dampers. Cycle-type mudguards were fitted to the first production Felbers, swivelling with the wheels when steering.

One day's production of Felbers parked in the works yard sometime in 1953. It may be surmised that this was a specially posed picture, with two of the cars already carrying registration plates. Today's total of surviving Felbers would probably be about equal to the number in this shot.

Felber & Co. supplied ten cars without bodywork to a specialist coachbuilder who finished them off in the form shown here, and sold them as the 'Möve 101' (Möve translates into English as Gull.) With wider and more sophisticated bodywork, the Möve was heavier and less stable. Performance and handling were inferior to the original, and the price was higher by more than 16 per cent in its home market. Despite the small number produced, one example survives to the present day in a Viennese museum.

At the end of 1953 Felber Autorollers had the bodywork modified at the front to accommodate fixed wings. This restored example belongs to Norbert Mylius of Vienna, and shows not only the full wings but also the bumper that was characteristic of late Felbers. Before the bumper was offered many owners were fitting new/old stock chromed bumpers originally made for Steyr Type 50 cars of the 1930s. Some cars were duotone-painted, and it is thought that the car shown here would originally have had the wings painted in a colour darker than the standard '*Nilgrün*' (Nile green) of the main body.

A press release towards the end of 1953 announced the introduction of the ultimate model, with full front wings. This wonderfully atmospheric photograph features the designer, Ernst Marold, and was produced as a part of the press pack. In 1993 Herr Marold autographed just eighty photographs to mark the fortieth anniversary of his creation. Note the width indicators on the wings, and the centrally mounted radio aerial.

A large contingent of Felber Autorollers, driven by members of the Austrian Autoroller Club, escorted the limousine carrying Ernst Marold and his bride following their wedding in 1954 at the Karlskirche, a Baroque cathedral in Vienna, a real indication of respect and affection that will never be repeated in these days of anonymous design teams working with computers to produce cars devoid of soul and character.

Felber Autorollers proved popular with drivers competing in the *Bergrennen* (uphill racing) near Vienna. In the early days of the event ultimate speed would decide the winner, but today, for historic vehicles, the results rely on achieving the same time in two or more attempts. Because of their three-wheel configuration, Felbers had to complete in the motorcycle and sidecar class, which explains the presence of a second person in each competing car. This shot shows a 1954 car ahead of one from the previous year, and was taken by the late Arthur Fenzlau at a race on 7 March 1954.

When Mr Felber died the company was divided up. Ernst Marold took over the part concentrating on the manufacture of industrial washing machines: this company still exists as part of the giant Electrolux group. Sadly the other arm of the company, making sidecars and trailers for motorcycles, failed – leading to the end of this line of Austrian vehicle manufacture.

CHAPTER SIX

WOBBLY DUCKS &
LITTLE HORSES

The history of the JARC remains something of an enigma. It is known that JARC Motors Ltd originally operated from a unit at premises owned by the Jarvis coachwork concern in Ladbroke Grove, London, a company established in 1886 producing the Jarvis 'Bicycle Made to Measure for Gentlemen'. One such gentleman to whom Jarvis supplied a bicycle was 'Charlie' Rolls who, as the Honourable C.S. Rolls, teamed up with Henry Royce to make and market the 'Best Car in the World'. Such was the respect for the craftsmanship of the Jarvis company that they subsequently built a number of bodies for Rolls-Royce cars, including most of those in the then fashionable style of the 'Balloon Body', the original example of which was built at the Derby factory of Rolls-Royce.

It was many years later, when a Mr Christoforedes approached Jarvis for the use of premises and other assistance, that the name JARC was born – Jar from Jarvis, combined with the initial letter C from Christoforedes. Jarvis were still involved with coachwork at the time, producing a number of car bodies for the Allard company, and it has been said that the style of the front panel for the production JARC vehicles is based loosely upon the outline of an Allard grille design.

The Ladbroke Grove site was also notable for being the home of possibly the first toddlers' toy to be manufactured commercially in Britain at the end of the Second World War. This was the 'Wobbly Duck', cut out of wood and fitted with wooden wheels, the mounting holes being drilled off-centre to produce the wobble. Each duck was painted (often blue), and a piece of string was attached so a child could pull it along.

The first JARC to leave the works is recalled as being of the same style as subsequent production models, with an angular van rear body and timber framework. Details of the car illustrated on this page, and the story behind its construction and presumed demise seem to have escaped unrecorded. A JARC sales brochure describes that production vehicle as the 'Little Horse Mark II', and it is a matter of conjecture whether this car might have been the intended 'Mark I'.

The JARC is usually said to have been available from about 1955, and as the registration number shown was issued in London in April 1954, the conclusion that it may have been used on pre-production models seems inescapable. At first glance the Mark II would appear to be the same vehicle with a simplified rear half, but in fact not one panel is common to both models. This little car, therefore, remains a mystery.

The production JARC Little Horse, designated Mark II (though the total production run must have been very small), is seen from these brochure illustrations to have undergone some radical re-design work. Note the use of the same registration number, and the presence on both this and the earlier example of road fund licence discs. Note also that the fuel filler, normally found in a central position on the front 'deck', appears to be absent from this picture.

The JARC was powered by a 250 cc air-cooled Excelsior twin-cylinder engine situated under the floor, just ahead of the rear axle, and driving through a Burman gearbox, then by chain to an axle with differential unit. With a payload of 364 lb (about 165 kg), and an average fuel consumption stated to be 65 mpg, it would have proved economical, though the manufacturer's claim that 'delivery by LITTLE HORSE can, under certain conditions, work out cheaper than delivery by bicycle' may have proved hard to justify. Supplied as a commercial vehicle, a single seat would have been standard specification, and the price was quoted as £347 16s 0d. A front passenger seat was available at extra cost as was 'provision . . . for carrying two small children' in the back.

By mid-1956 the British Anzani Engineering Company Limited had taken over production of the JARC, and had re-christened it the Astra. British Anzani, whose roots spread back to 1912, when they represented the British arm of the Italian-based Anzani Engine Company, had a multi-faceted history. During the First World War they produced aero engines, subsequently moving on to car and motorcycle engines. Following a re-structuring of the company in 1927, they concentrated upon development work for outside organisations. By 1938 Charles Harrison had become managing director – he had previously been technical director of the British Motor Boat Manufacturing Company, whose business also took in the manufacture of fairground roundabouts and dodgem cars, with which Mr Harrison planned to compete (see page 90).

Deliveries began today of the ASTRA, a new British economy runabout, being tried out here by 19-year-old SUSAN FLYNN in London.

The smallest and cheapest four-wheeler on the British Market, it has all-round independent suspension, hydraulic brakes and a rear-mounted twin-cylinder engine. Costing £347 16s 0d, including purchase tax, it has the appearance of a station wagon and can carry two people and up to 250-pounds of goods or luggage.

It has a 322 cc twin-cylinder two-stroke engine giving a top speed of 55 mph and an average fuel consumption of 60 miles per gallon.'

Outboard marine engines formed the bulk of the company's output after the Second World War, and they entered the motorcycle engine field in 1953 with 250 cc and 322 cc twin-cylinder two-stroke engines, which were supplied to a number of companies. The Astra offered an opportunity to produce their own vehicle utilising the 322 cc version of the engine produced in-house. The public announcement of the new Astra took the form of a selection of photographs showing this car, with accompanying press releases. It is noteworthy that 57 JMK already differed from the brochure illustration in certain details. Observe the absence of bumpers (listed elsewhere as an extra cost option) and the wing-mounted badge bearing the legend 'Hampton Hill, Middlesex, ASTRA'. Evidently pleated skirts and sleeveless tops were the fashion in 1956.

'19-year-old Susan Flynn removing the spare wheel from its housing under the bonnet', says the press release. One wonders why Miss Flynn's age was reported in such detail. Perhaps it was her birthday. . . .

Although the 57 JMK registration number can be clearly seen (earlier picture), it is interesting to record that advertisements for the Astra were appearing as late as 1959, using the old OYE 20 number inherited from JARC. Like its predecessor the JARC, the Astra was never a good seller, and by 1959 it was no longer advertised. However there is evidence that cars could still be supplied as late as 1960 in 'knocked-down form for home assembly' at just £190, or less body parts for £155. A quick calculation indicates that the complete body assembly was costed at a mere £35!

Salvaged from a scrapyard in Oxfordshire in 1979, this complete chassis/engine would surely benefit from the addition of one of the £35 bodyshells mentioned previously!

The JARC/Astra story closes with Astra production and sales being transferred to Gill Getabout Cars of Paddington. The company claimed to have embarked on vehicle production as early as 1891, but this was a short-lived flirtation. The Gill craftsmen produced two designs of car, both using the inherited Astra chassis and mechanical components. The Coupé featured a wrap-around plastic rear screen and some interesting styling.

It has been said that the Getabout was also to be made in a form that would enable it to be used as a taxi. With Public Carriage Office regulations covering minimum dimensions for such vehicles, it seems unlikely that the Gill product could have been made to conform. Sadly there are no records of any surviving Gill Getabout cars. Note the same registration number on both Gill demonstration vehicles.

The dodgem cars produced by the British Motor Boat Manufacturing Company at their King's Cross premises had led to a brief but fascinating flirtation with microcars during the 1930s when the company boss, Jack Shillan, realised that it would be possible to use a petrol-engined version on the road. Christened the Rytecraft Scoota-car, several types were built, all of them styled as conventional cars but in miniature. The first, launched in 1934, was powered by a Villiers 98 cc engine and had a top speed of just 15 mph. Three years later a more sophisticated version, similar to that illustrated here with its Australian owner, was available with a 250 cc engine and could top 40 mph!

Commercial van and truck versions followed, and a few were even styled as miniatures of Vauxhall and Chrysler Airflow cars. Surprisingly, sixty years on, several examples of Rytecraft Scoota-car are known to survive, and one with the original 98 cc engine even took its owner, the late Jim Parkinson, on a (slow) trip round the world in 1965.

CHAPTER SEVEN

GLASSFIBRE MOULDING APPROACHES ITS ZENITH

The satisfactory results that were being achieved with glassfibre reinforced plastics highlighted the very real advantages of such materials for vehicles where very lengthy production runs could not realistically be anticipated. With fibreglass as the manufacturing medium, there was no reason, other than the cost of the initial mould, why one-off bodies could not be produced. The material was also easy, though messy, to use and to repair. It could have a pigment added at the mixing stage to ensure density of colour, meaning that minor scratches appeared less unsightly, and comparatively intricate contours were simple to form. Added to all these, it permitted the construction of lightweight, yet strong and resilient body structures with the minimum of expensive plant.

The MVM, Tourette, and Scootacar were but three of a multitude of fibreglass-bodied microcars to appear in the 1950s. Others included the Berkeley, the Frisky and the Nobel in England, and a plethora of European makes.

One of the more unusual locations for a prospective motor car manufacturer must surely be Guernsey, yet it was on that Island in the Sun that Leslie Le Tissier, owner of Manor View Motor Works, devised his plan to build the MVM sports car in 1955. A prototype was built and road tested, with encouraging results. Acceleration was reported in the *Guernsey Evening Press* as being 'astounding', and the four-wheel independent suspension 'excellent'. The prototype car, registered in Guernsey with the number Z 81, is shown as tested, but still awaiting decorative chromed mouldings.

Mr Le Tissier announced that he was planning to employ about fifteen local men and to commence production of about five or six cars a week. These would then be exported to England for sale.

With the then popular choice of British Anzani 322 cc engine, the MVM should have provided competition for the Berkeley of the period, though the separate chassis would have made it inherently more rigid. A top speed in the region of 65 mph was envisaged, and the price was to have been about £350 ex-works. An additional and larger model was planned, capable of 100 mph. Sadly production never commenced, and the only two MVM cars known to have been completed seem to have become extinct, although the chassis of one is said to have been used by Frank Cohu as the basis for a sand-racing car in 1962.

The long-established garage business of Carr Bros, situated at Purley, Surrey, became home to the cheapest three-wheeler then available when, in 1956, they set about producing the Tourette. A.J.P. Merkelt, already Service and Workshop Controller, originated the Tourette concept and was appointed Chief Designer. He first designed a simple chassis upon which was to be mounted a choice of body, either coach-built aluminium on ash frame, or fibreglass, moulded in upper and lower halves and bonded at the waist. A prototype chassis was built and mated to a Villiers 8E engine, and this was made available for inspection by the press. The only apparent criticism seems to have concerned the steering, which was altered before the commencement of production to incorporate a modified Standard 8 steering box.

An early suggestion of Tourette styling indicated that the headlamps would be recessed into the body as shown here, but production cars had them mounted above the body contour, where they detracted from the smooth lines but were more easily accessible for maintenance, and probably more effective. The casual observer would probably have had difficulty in ascertaining which method of construction had been used for the bodywork, since it was reported that the first coachbuilt body would, in fact, be used as a former for the mould which would produce the fibreglass units, thus ensuring a near identical appearance.

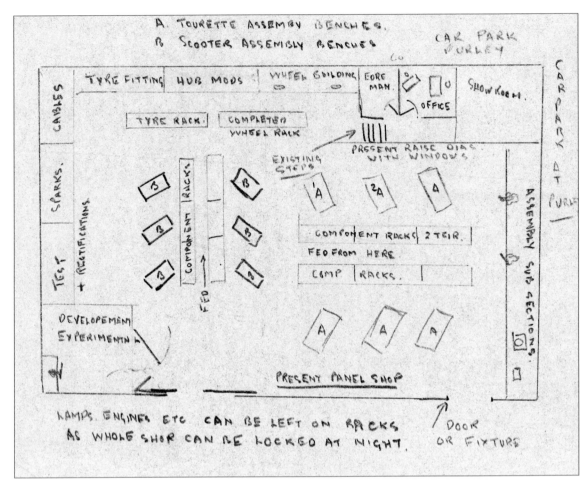

The prototype example having been thoroughly tested by the makers of its Villiers power unit, a subsidiary company, The Progress Supreme Company Ltd, was formed. Carr Bros, actually owned by the impressively named Cornishman Tresleyan Jasper Thomas following the death of Major Carr, had already been involved with the marketing of the Dutch-built Hostaco three-wheeler and Progress and Parilla motor scooters from Germany and Italy respectively, but the major step was taken to anglicise the entire range of scooters and produce them on site alongside the Tourette, all to be sold under the brand name Progress. A sketch of the proposed layout for the fabrication and assembly shop – previously the Carr Bros panel shop – indicates scope for only limited scale production.

The Scooters became known as the Britannia, the Briton and the Anglian, with varying mechanical specifications, each employing a different model of Villiers engine.

By February 1957 the Tourette had developed into a range of three models. The Junior, with a flat windscreen and cloth hood, was priced at just £229 10s 0d (plus £58 10s 6d tax, making a total of only £288 0s 6d), well below the price of any competitor. The Senior and Deluxe models both featured bright plastic hoods with curved windscreens but the Deluxe could be supplied in any choice of dual-tone colour schemes from a stock range, and included transparent side-screens, spare wheel and tyre, ornamental wheel covers, luggage grid and direction indicators in the specification. No subsequent mention was made of the coachbuilt version, and the windscreen options henceforth became fully interchangeable between models.

With its ovoid appearance and waistline bonding, the Tourette bears a resemblance to some of the designs of Egon Brütsch in Germany, but as Mr Merkelt was unaware of the work of Brütsch, the similarity was purely coincidental and the whole car was an original Merkelt design, though the front hubs and wheels were sourced from the Messerschmitt KR 200 for which Carr Bros also held an agency. Practical assistance at the design stage was provided by Arthur Chaproniere, the Works Foreman.

A comprehensive selection of extras was available to the Tourette owner, including this 'Cabin Top', which hinged forward for entry and egress. The absence of conventional doors would have served the dual functions of simplifying the design and therefore reducing costs, and increasing structural rigidity. Other accessories ranged from a 'Superior (Loud Note)' electric horn and a 'Phillips Fit Yourself' 4-valve radio to a 'Larger Battery' – presumably to compensate for excessive use of the two former items! There was even the option of a hand-operated clutch for disabled drivers – though how they would actually get into the car is open to speculation.

Driving the Tourette has been recalled as '. . . an experience not to be forgotten. Operation of the brakes on wet or icy road conditions would result in the vehicle rotating rapidly. Failure of a front tyre would result in the vehicle moving rapidly towards the side of the road on which the tyre had failed, even if the steering was full lock in the other direction.' The designer's son himself recalls that 'if the vehicle were used by a driver without a passenger to act as a counter balance, turning hard left at speed would result in the vehicle turning over. I did survive such an event with only twelve stitches in my right thigh and the loss of a new suit.' The car concerned also survived – see above. Most of these criticisms would probably have applied equally to many other three-wheeled microcars of the period, but the Tourette's extreme lightness probably exacerbated the situation somewhat.

An interesting aside to the story of the Tourette concerns the Car-ette Supreme. This was to have been built and sold alongside the Tourette and would have shared many components, but official publicity describes the Car-ette as a '3-wheeled 2-seater (in line) Coupé, with hinged opening part-transparent top. Designed along the general lines of the Continental Cabin Scooters which have recently come into favour'. It would, therefore, appear that the aim was to produce a British rival to the Messerschmitt. Prices were stated as being £262 15s 0d plus £66 19s 9d purchase tax for the Standard model, and £278 15s 0d plus £71 1s 4d for the Deluxe, which latter version offered 'Spare Wheel, Heater, Wheel Discs (otherwise "Extras"), Dual-tone ornamental finish'. The basic colour was to be Saxe Blue, but alternatives could be arranged to order. Despite this wealth of detail, the Car-ette did not progress beyond the concept stage, and no trace of production remains.

Scootacars Limited was an offshoot of the Hunslet Engine Company, an old-established manufacturer of railway locomotives situated, not really surprisingly, in the Leeds suburb of Hunslet. It was here that Henry Brown – previously associated with the Rodley car – produced the original design for one of the more successful purely British microcars. To produce the basic shape, it is said that Mr Brown sketched the outline of a Villiers 9E two-stroke engine with himself seated directly above it, and fitted everything else around. The result was a car that had the appearance of being disproportionately tall but very narrow. In reality the car was wider than it looked, with a surprisingly low centre of gravity. The basis for the car was a steel chassis and floorpan, with the well-tried Villiers 9E engine situated amidships driving the rear wheel, and direct steering controlled by a handlebar.

On to the completed chassis was grafted a robust fibreglass body, made in left and right halves with the join running up the front panel, along the roof and down the back. A single door was fitted, on the left side, and this gave access to accommodation for two people – and perhaps an occasional third. The power unit was tucked away inside an inverted metal box, with a longitudinal bench seat on top. Halfway back was a removable back rest for the driver, with the passenger sitting astride the bench but to the rear. This arrangement dispensed with the need for a separate engine bay, and gave the Scootacar a foreshortened appearance leading to comparisons with contemporary telephone kiosks – particularly since many Scootacars were finished in red.

With testing of the prototype completed, production commenced in the second half of 1957, the only obvious change being to the rear window, where the pillars were enlarged for increased rigidity. Soon, Scootacars were being assembled in increasing numbers. This view of the Scootacar assembly shop shows the hand-built nature of the process typical of most smaller car manufacturing operations.

Once built up to a rolling form, cars were returned to floor level, turned around and pushed back along the workshop for finishing and checking. Note the door and windows at the end of the building, so typical of railway works throughout the country – though Hunslet's were a private concern, rather than part of a railway company.

Completed Scootacars were parked outside the Jack Lane premises to await dispatch. Normal colour choices were red, ivory or light blue, with a contrasting colour for the interior. The wider rear screen pillars gave production Scootacars a slightly less upright appearance . . . but everything is relative. The windscreen was of safety glass, but the rear screen and side windows – made to slide open for ventilation – were perspex.

On a wet day in 1958 this Scootacar prepares to become airborne at the Motor Industry Research Association test track. Contrary to ill-informed opinion, the Scootacar was very stable and possessed good handling characteristics. 7016 U was registered by Scootacars in January 1958, but nothing is known of its subsequent history.

Despite its modest proportions, the Scootacar incorporated ample space for the carriage of personal effects, with one of the largest front parcel trays to be found on any make or model of car, additional space out of sight in a separate compartment beneath the front seat, and masses of floor space. The spare wheel was carried out of the way on the rear panel, and there was even a moulded pocket in the door. This delightful Yorkshire lass seems to have chanced upon a hat box on the roadside verge.

Nel and Peter Motte undertook a journey to Istanbul by Scootacar in 1959, many miles of which involved traversing unmade tracks really not fit to be deemed roads. Besides themselves, they loaded into their car a tent, air beds and sleeping bags, typewriter, photographic outfit, tape recorder, cooking utensils (including a petrol Primus stove), spares, personal effects for three months, and 2 gallons of oil! The car performed well but had to be abandoned following a head-on collision with a bicycle(!) on the return journey. The Mottes subsequently wrote a book about the trip, entitled *Balkan Roads to Istanbul*.

Production of the Scootacar well under way, it was decided that there was scope for a more refined model. Unusually the specification of the Deluxe, announced in 1960, was not achieved by simply adding a few items of trim, but was brought about by a complete restyling of the vehicle. Because of this it is usually referred to as the Mark 2. Style had come to the Scootacar.

Within the new car was a revised seating arrangement. With the engine now tucked away beneath the rear seat, which was wide enough to accommodate two smallish people in comparative comfort, the driver's seat and controls were offset slightly to the right, and the seat could be tipped forward to permit passengers ease of access. Sadly, though there is no doubt that the Scootacar Deluxe was a very sound car, it appeared too late to achieve substantial sales.

It had been anticipated from the very beginning that a more powerful engine unit might be made available as an option. This came to pass in 1961, when a Villiers twin-cylinder engine of 250 cc was fitted to the first of a small number of examples that were designated the Scootacar Twin. The rare Twin model has passed into folklore as the Mark 3, and it was, in all other respects, identical to the Deluxe. Of a total production of about 1,500 Scootacars, probably only about fifty had the twin-cylinder engine. Production of Scootacars ended in 1965, but a measure of their durability can be determined from the high survival rate.

CHAPTER EIGHT

A FROTH OF BUBBLES

True bubblecars were a product of Continental thinking, yet were very much fashion accessories in Britain as well as providing inexpensive transport. It has been stated elsewhere that these quirky little machines were the result of the 1956 Suez crisis, but with the Italian Iso Isetta appearing in 1953, and the Messerschmitt and Heinkel following in rapid succession, this is clearly not the case.

Bubblecars were raced and rallied. They travelled to the most obscure regions. They were sold all over the globe. Many were photographed with or owned by show-business celebrities. Others appeared on the silver screen themselves. And they were often loved and pampered by their owners.

In modern times bubblecars have acquired cult status. Their values have increased manyfold. But they remain what they always were – some of the most ingenious vehicles ever invented.

Although most people associate the Isetta with BMW, and rightly so, it was the Italian company responsible for the manufacture of Isotherm refrigerators who originally had the foresight to take Ermenegildo Preti's revolutionary design from the drawing board to the streets in 1953. The company was owned by Renzo Rivolta, and had already entered the automotive market with the Iso motor-scooter. From 1962 the company made high-performance GT cars, the first of which took the company owner's surname as its identity – the Iso Rivolta.

Preti's original design needed but little modification before the first production cars, using an unconventional power unit with two pistons in a common combustion chamber, were made available. Like most subsequent derivatives, the cars were entered through a large opening panel at the front, and there were twin rear wheels placed close enough together to dispense with the need for a differential. Although production is said to have continued until 1956, both at home in Italy and under licence in Belgium, the Italians never seemed prepared to pay the relatively high purchase price, preferring to stick with their nippy little Vespa scooters or economical Fiat cars.

Alongside the Isetta – literally 'Little Iso' – a small number of commercial variants were produced, including this Autocarro 500 truck (some had tipping bodies and there was even a fire engine), the original illustration of which shows the conventional rear axle with differential. The figure of 500 in the model designation is thought to reflect the payload in kilogrammes. One can well imagine the Autocarro in use with a small jobbing builder . . .

Autofurgone 500

. . . while this very smart Autofurgone 500 would surely not be out of place carrying exclusive fashion garments around the streets of Milan. Such a smart and apparently well-finished body would have added considerably to the weight. Low gearing to overcome this would have resulted in a top speed that the average Italian driver may have found hard to accept. Unlikely as it seems, it is thought that this commercial version of the original Iso Isetta is, happily, not extinct.

The setting sun casts a long shadow over the finishing line as the flag drops to the cheers of the crowd at the end of a gruelling 1,000-mile drive.

It may seem remarkable that the Iso company would even have considered entering a team of their diminutive cars in the 1954 Mille Miglia race. All the more remarkable, though, is that all four cars entered the following year completed the course, winning the 'Index of Performance' for their class at an average speed of almost 80 kph, ahead of Citroën! The author wonders how long the marshal had been patiently waiting there to bring down the chequered flag on this entrant.

Note the headlights situated low down on the front 'wings', and the vertically mounted door handle, characteristic of Isettas of the Iso type. The driver is wearing a helmet, but other protective measures are conspicuous by their absence.

Throughout Europe entrepreneurs were coming to the fore with schemes that were intended to bring motoring to the masses, and this was particularly true in Germany, which was, in the early 1950s, a country attempting to rebuild not only its towns and cities but also its industries and the morale of the people. The Italian Isetta had caught the imagination of several forward-thinking businessmen, among them Jakob Hoffmann. The Hoffmann factory had already been producing motor-cycles and scooters, and he even had his own 250 cc horizontally opposed engine readily available. When the Isetta came to his attention he realised it could prove to be the stepping stone from small-scale producer of two-wheeled transport to the expanding field of car manufacture. Failing in his attempt to acquire a licence for production in Germany, he instructed his designers to adapt the Isetta concept, but with sufficient differences for it to be considered a separate vehicle. The result was the vehicle illustrated here, the Hoffmann Auto-Kabine 250.

The similarity to the Isetta is quite startling, apart from the fundamental difference that the Hoffmann was equipped with a single rear-hinged door on the right-hand (passenger) side. The car was powered by Hoffmann's engine and interior accommodation was limited to a bench seat.

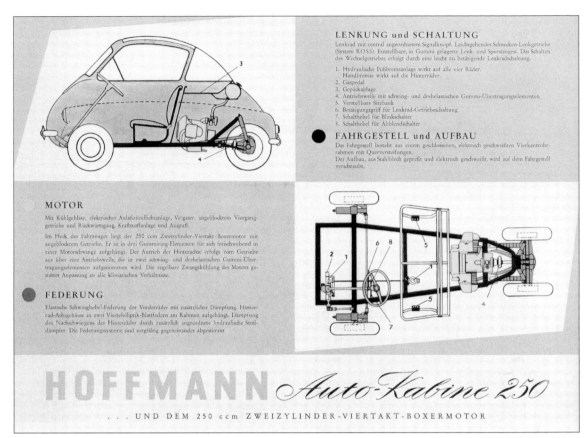

LENKUNG und SCHALTUNG

Lenkrad mit zentral angeordnetem Signalknopf. Leichtgehendes Schnecken-Lenkgetriebe (System ROSS). Einstellbare, in Gummi gelagerte Lenk- und Spurstangen. Das Schalten des Wechselgetriebes erfolgt durch eine leicht zu betätigende Lenkradschaltung.

1. Hydraulische Fußbremsanlage wirkt auf alle vier Räder.
   Handbremse wirkt auf die Hinterräder.
2. Gaspedal
3. Gepäckablage
4. Antriebswelle mit schwing- und drehelastischen Gummi-Übertragungselementen
5. Verstellbare Sitzbank
6. Betätigungsgriff für Lenkrad-Getriebeschaltung
7. Schalthebel für Blinkschalter
8. Schalthebel für Abblendschalter

FAHRGESTELL und AUFBAU

Das Fahrgestell besteht aus einem geschlossenen, elektrisch geschweißten Vierkantrohrrahmen mit Querverteifungen.
Der Aufbau, aus Stahlblech gepreßt und elektrisch geschweißt, wird auf dem Fahrgestell verschraubt.

MOTOR

Mit Kühlgebläse, elektrischer Anlaßzündlichtanlage, Vergaser, angeblocktem Viergang-getriebe und Rückwärtsgang, Kraftstoffanlage und Auspuff.

Im Heck des Fahrzeuges liegt der 250 ccm Zweizylinder-Viertakt-Boxermotor mit angeblocktem Getriebe. Er ist in drei Gummiring-Elementen für sich freischwebend in einer Motorschwinge aufgehängt. Der Antrieb der Hinterachse erfolgt vom Getriebe aus über eine Antriebswelle, die in zwei schwing- und drehelastischen Gummi-Übertragungselementen aufgenommen wird. Die regelbare Zwangskühlung des Motors gestattet Anpassung an alle klimatischen Verhältnisse.

FEDERUNG

Elastische Schwinghebel-Federung der Vorderräder mit zusätzlicher Dämpfung. Hinterrad-Achsgehäuse in zwei Viertelelliptik-Blattfedern am Rahmen aufgehängt. Dämpfung des Nachschwingens der Hinterräder durch zusätzlich angeordnete hydraulische Stoßdämpfer. Die Federungssysteme sind sorgfältig gegeneinander abgestimmt.

HOFFMANN *Auto-Kabine 250*

... UND DEM 250 ccm ZWEIZYLINDER-VIERTAKT-BOXERMOTOR

Two prototypes were unveiled to the press on 2 June 1954, with Hoffmann claiming any similarity between his car and the Isetta product were mere coincidence. Delivery of production Hoffmann cars, available in either Standard or Luxus versions, commenced just three months later, in September of the same year. By this time, though, BMW had successfully negotiated the rights to produce their own version of the Isetta in Germany, and a court action was commenced to force Hoffmann to discontinue production.

By the time legal proceedings were finalised, not only was Hoffmann's dream of being a car manufacturer in ruins but so was his company. The last of 113 Hoffmann cars was completed in February 1955, and the business went into liquidation the following month. It is said that all unsold stocks of Hoffmann Kabines were destroyed, and there certainly seems little likelihood of any examples surviving today.

With the embarrassing Hoffmann debacle
out of the way, BMW were gearing up for
Isetta production in Germany. The
Munich company were satisfied with the
overall concept but had a reputation to
maintain, so set about incorporating
certain improvements, starting with the
substitution of a modified version of one
of their existing four-stroke motorcycle
engines for the somewhat unusual
Italian two-stroker. This shot, used in
a very early BMW Isetta brochure, shows
a possibly unique car, before final
evolution into its production form.

The first BMW Isettas, still recognisable as a descendant of the Iso, went on sale in April of 1955,
and proved an immediate success. The earliest models can be identified by their quarter bumpers at
the front, the long tapering headlight nacelles faired in just above the waist line, and the pear-
shaped indicators midway along the sides. In this view can be seen the remnants of ISO features
such as the door handle and wheel discs.

The success of the Isetta in its first year encouraged BMW to make a number of detail alterations as well as offering extras for 1956. Among the former were the adoption of safety glass instead of 'Plexiglass' acrylic side windows, the substitution of rectangular indicator lamps and simpler headlamp housings. The extras included aluminium mouldings and the option of two-tone paint finishes for those purchasers who demanded a bit more panache, and luggage racks for fitting to the interior parcel shelf or the rear exterior. Whichever was used, rearward visibility was compromised, so additional mirrors were popular.

The needs of the small businessman were not overlooked. Without too great a capital outlay BMW managed to attach a platform for the carriage of goods in place of the rear window and luggage area. Either box or open versions were offered, but both were only really suitable for goods that were neither bulky nor heavy.

Overseas sales of Isettas, always modified to suit local requirements, added to the success story. USA market models received extra bumpers and different lighting and signalling arrangements, and their introduction in 1956 was accompanied by this brochure. German licensing conditions favoured vehicles with engines of less than 250 cc, but Isettas destined for export were generally of 295 cc displacement.

A. LOUIS STRAUS
"A Good Name Means A Good Deal"
127 E. 12th Street
ERIE, PA.   Phone 23-495

NOW... EUROPE'S HIT CAR IS HERE

From 1958 BMW offered an Isetta with a more modern outline to the glazed area. In place of swivelling quarter windows the front windows would slide open, resulting in more controllable ventilation. At the same time the front suspension was re-designed. For a while both body styles were sold side by side, with the 'bubble-window' being sold as the Standard, and the 'sliding-window' being designated the Export. Another USA brochure shows clearly the extra bumpers, high-mounted rear turn signals and a simplified waist moulding.

The enterprising Berlin coachbuilding concern of Buhne constructed their own more stylish variation on the Isetta van theme. Few were actually made, and none at all are likely to have survived.

It is not clear whether the fuel filler has been repositioned from its usual place below the rear window, or whether topping up with petrol would necessitate the removal of the payload.

With the removal of the cargo tray, and substitution of a fold-down hood, BMW found they had an instant convertible on their hands. The 'tropical' door conversion was available for hot climates. With door vents and windows open, sunroof back and hood down, sunshine was there for all to enjoy.

The US market was the target of much Isetta advertising, with well-known personalities including Cary Grant attempting to add to the little car's credibility. In fact, of those Americans who did buy, it seems likely that a large percentage – including Elvis Presley – recalled the cars from their military days based in Germany serving 'Uncle Sam'. For the record, Miss Rheingold was elected annually by the customers of the Liebmann brewery in New York. The contest followed on from the 1940 trading year, when Jinx Falkenburg was chosen by company president Philip Liebmann to promote the brewery's products. Miss Rheingold of 1958 was Madelyn Darrow. The contest ended in 1964, when Celeste Yarnall polled the most votes. Selection by the company returned in 1965, but this was the finale for Miss Rheingold. The contest was big business for a quarter of a century, attracting more local interest than the presidential elections. The 1959 winner, successor to Miss Darrow, polled twenty-two million votes!

This mail-franking postmark was used for a short time in the USA. Enlargement from its original size of about 3 cm × 2.5 cm reveals it to show a German-made sliding window four-wheeler with tropical door, two-tone paint and US fittings.

The total production of BMW Isettas was in excess of 160,000, with the last coming off the production line in May 1962. They gave good service and were a familiar sight in towns and cities throughout Germany. This Munich street scene shows three sliding-window types and an early bubble-window (far right) negotiating heavy two- and four-wheeled traffic.

In recent years an enthusiastic following has built up in countries throughout the world, but it was not always thus. Such a small vehicle was found to be unsuited to the highways of America and many examples were abandoned. The Sadwin family rescued this low-mileage 1956 bubble-window model from a New England junkyard in 1980 'to give it a happy home'.

With the overwhelming success of BMW in producing and marketing Isettas, Iso ceased production in their own plants in 1956. Total Iso output for that year has been reported as being a mere seventeen units and production was given over to a light truck of more conventional design. The tooling from the Italian and Belgian Iso operations – it could scarcely be regarded as being worn out – was shipped over to Brazil, where it was used by Americo Emilio Romi's company to make the Romi-Isetta Tourisme.

This photograph, taken in 1956, shows Señor Romi and his wife Olympia in one of the first cars to bear the family name. Gathered round are members of the Romi family, and in the background there are more cars on the production line.

This colourful sales brochure shows that the cars were made under licence from ISO SpA. A careful study of the original also reveals that most of the illustrations contained therein were lifted directly from ISO literature.

Initial car production also duplicated that of the ISO range, but later cars – designated Romi-Isetta 300 Deluxe – were fitted with the more conventional BMW motor. This example, photographed in about 1978, was owned by Americo's grandson Claudio Romi Zanaga of São Paolo, and had undergone a thorough restoration.

Just as BMW acquired the rights to build the Isetta in Germany, so did VELAM (Véhicule léger à Moteur) come to a similar arrangement in France. However, whereas the German car underwent only relatively minor adaptations, the Gallic version was startlingly different. Not only was the bodyshell redesigned, but it was a monocoque, rather than being dependent upon a separate chassis. The engine/transmission unit – always with twin rear wheels – was mounted on a bolted-on subframe.

Typical of Gallic practice, the wheels were attached with only three studs each, and were of the unusual 11-inch diameter. Within the car little trace of the Iso remained. A couple of odd touches concerned the speedometer, which on most Isettas was the only dial on the instrument panel, but which was mounted in the centre of the VELAM steering wheel, and the push-button door release ahead of the headlamp – note the absence of a conventional handle. Perhaps the photographer was unaware that the windscreen wiper was intended to sweep only the glass!

117

Competing with the oh-so-practical Citroën 2CV and the pretty Renault 750, the VELAM never attracted the hoped-for sales success. A refined version, with further substantial modifications, and designated the Ecrin model, did little to improve the situation, and VELAM gave up the unequal struggle in 1959. Where the basic VELAM Isetta had adopted a redesign of the lower body, the Ecrin used a different superstructure, too.

Not everybody was unimpressed, though. Lincoln International Limited made a plastic toy VELAM 'with powerful gyro motor', measuring 9 centimetres in length, a must for every enthusiast, and the Ewbank picture card set 'Miniature Cars & Scooters' included this picture, with the note that 'This model was fully silenced in 1958'! The blacked-out rear window area suggests that the picture actually represented the 'Décapotable' version, with fold-down hood – a rare beast indeed.

It was in the redundant locomotive works at the London, Brighton and South Coast Railway that Captain Ronnie Ashley set up the production line for Isetta of Great Britain Limited. Unusually for a car factory there was no direct road access, although pedestrians could negotiate a flight of steps to enter. The late Vic Locke, who became a founder member of the Isetta Owners' Club of Great Britain, reported that on the occasion of his initial visit the workforce was on strike and the place was deserted. All parts and materials had to be shipped in by rail, and completed Isettas were dispatched in the same manner – even those that were destined for dealers in the same town!

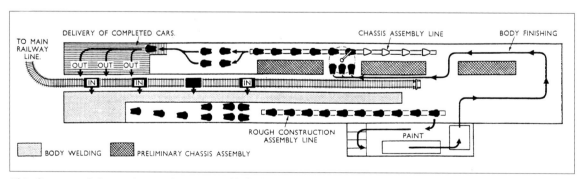

This diagram of the production line was published to accompany a report of the start of production in 1957 in *The Motor*. The same article pointed out that an order for 1,000 Isettas for Canada was to be fulfilled. Whereas BMW of Germany were supplying the United States, only English production was acceptable in the Dominion of Canada.

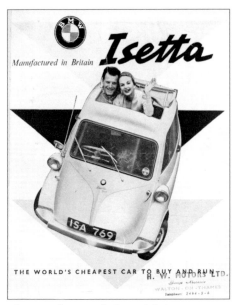

The car illustrated above left is not quite what it seems. This 1957 brochure for the newly introduced British Isetta was designed and printed by the firm of Samson Clark & Co Ltd, who are to be congratulated on their expertise with regard to the re-use of illustrations. Observe the happy couple here with their smart new Isetta. How were they to know that the very car in which they were posing had previously been seen with tropical door vents . . . or was it the other way around? It would seem that the car used for the pictures was, in reality, a German model (see the German indicators and mirror) that was being used to evaluate various design features prior to commencing production at Brighton. Note the odd three-piece arrangement of bumper, using quarter bumpers similar to the 1955 type, with a central section attached to the door. The letter I was never used for English registration numbers, so the number shown was obviously false.

The first British-built (as distinct from British-supplied) Isettas took the form of right-hand-drive four-wheelers with engines of 295 cc, and so were not ideally suited to the British market, where they were included in the same classification as conventional cars and subject to the same road tax, whereas three-wheeled competitors were regarded as tricycles, attracting a lower rate of tax. The tricycle had the added advantage that, provided it was rendered incapable of reversing – a simple matter – it could lawfully be driven by anyone unaccompanied holding just a provisional motorcycle licence. This example is owned and enjoyed in sunny Australia.

It was a relatively simple matter to create a three-wheeled Isetta by the expedient of a re-design of the final drive assembly. By reverting to a left-hand-drive arrangement, the weight distribution was kept fairly equal, with the driver on the left to balance the effect of the engine on the right. This prevented any untoward tendency for the car to topple over on left turns. Brian Westoby's car, above, has covered over a quarter of a million miles, and was photographed at an early Burford microcar rally.

The Isetta only achieved full acceptability in Britain when a right-hand-drive version with three wheels became available. All the major component parts were already in production, but it was only by fitting a cast-iron weight low down on the left side of the car, concealed by the interior trim panel, that stability when driving could be assured, and production of the new model set in motion. All this happened in about 1959, just as most of the unsold stock of Canadian cars were arriving back at the works. It is thought that they were converted to British (but LHD) specification and released to the home market. The single front bumper blade was characteristic of Brighton-built 'Plus' models from about 1961.

British-made Isettas were built on chassis units fabricated by Rubery Owen at Birmingham, but used bodyshells brought in from BMW. Braking was by Girling, and the lighting was the preserve of Lucas. Tyre sizes differed, being of 4.40 × 10 inches on German cars, but 4.80 × 10 inches on the Brighton product, with 5.20 × 10 inches specified for the rear of the three-wheeler. On all types the door was hinged on the driver's side, with the steering column jointed at the base to allow the wheel to swing away when the door opened. This car was owned by Mike Bray of Sussex. He had bought it as a wreck and just completed restoration when it was used for this 1981 Dunlop calendar illustration. Dunlop was the sole supplier of tyres to Isetta GB Ltd.

The picture shows that this car is a 'standard' model, with smaller (5 inch) headlamps, and without bumpers of any description.

The English Isetta was alone in offering two-pedal transmission, using the Smith's Selectroshift system. This, unlike completely automatic transmissions using torque converters, did not absorb engine power, but simply replaced the pedal-operated clutch with one based upon magnetic powder activated when the gearshift lever was gripped. Few Isettas were so equipped. The registration number seems somewhat familiar.

Isetta

. . . USE

ISA 769

SMITHS
SELECTROSHIFT

REVOLUTIONARY 2 PEDAL SYSTEM WITH MAGNETIC POWDER COUPLING

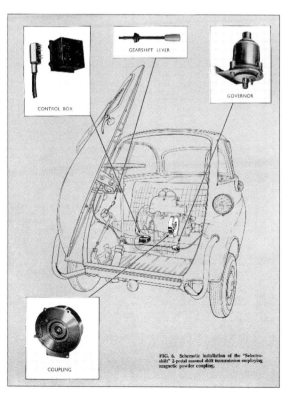

CONTROL BOX

GEARSHIFT LEVER

GOVERNOR

COUPLING

FIG. 6. Schematic installation of the "Selectroshift" 2-pedal manual shift transmission employing magnetic powder coupling.

The Smith's Selectroshift system as fitted to an Isetta. This illustration, first published in 1957, shows the major components of the system, and their positions in relation to the normal car.

With the commonality of major components between German and English Isettas, it was perhaps inevitable that the commercial version would eventually emerge from the Brighton works. The RAC used a small fleet until they were ousted in favour of Austin A35 and Mini vans. Notice how old-style trafficators have been fitted to the leading corner of the luggage box. Notice also Patrolman Isherwood's strange attire, perhaps suitable for the Norton motorcycle that would have been his previous steed, but not quite the thing for an Isetta. The tubular bumpers are typical of Isetta 'Plus' models made at Brighton in about 1959.

Another van, but this one retains its Lucas flashers midway along the side. The absence of bumpers identifies this as a standard model. Whether it was used for deliveries or merely as an advertisement is not known. The registration indicates use in Guernsey. The rear load space could carry 165 lbs, with a further 187 lbs carried alongside the single seat. A mesh barrier was installed to protect the driver from his load.

Although the extra-cost option of Selectroshift transmission did not prove popular, it was reliable and would have been ideally suited to this Isetta version intended for supply to disabled drivers. The passenger side of the seat was on runners, so the disabled driver could shuffle across, then propel him- or herself forward to the edge of the car to alight. The project seems to have been still-born, with companies such as AC, Invacar, Barrett, Stanley and Tippen supplying the majority of disabled driver cars, to Health Ministry specifications.

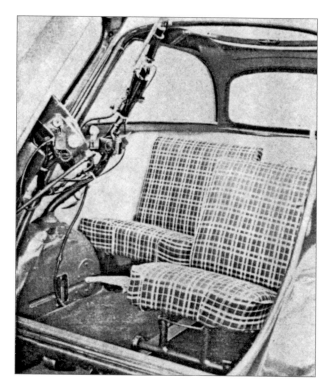

In Germany, too, they were aware of the special needs of the disabled driver, but their solution was simpler. This 1955 bubble-window BMW Isetta was fitted with hand controls linked to the normal pedals. The seat appears to be fixed, but a stool was supplied for the driver to lower himself on to before moving back on to the seat. This arrangement was an after-market conversion to a standard Isetta, rather than a separate model.

Another still-born Isetta product was this fibreglass-bodied van, which was advertised as having a 4 cwt payload. It is said to have remained at the works for some time, but its ultimate fate seems shrouded in mystery.

Bubble cars have sometimes performed duties above and beyond what was originally expected of them. During the 'Cold War' two German Isettas were secretly modified to provide concealed – and very cramped – accommodation beneath the rear parcel shelves, alongside the engines. The purpose was to smuggle escapees past East German border guards, on the assumption that no-one would imagine it possible to carry a stowaway in such a small vehicle. The car shown here on display in a Berlin museum made six successful trips. The other car was searched and the 57-year-old woman occupant discovered after she made a movement while the driver's papers were being inspected at the checkpoint on its fourth trip. On a less sombre note, Graham Parsons, a south London musician, bought a second-hand Isetta from a Chinese pianist living in Surbiton, and once used it to transport jazz drummer Phil Seaman (plus his drum kit!) to Ronnie Scott's club in London, where he was to perform. On another occasion, Tubby Hayes occupied the passenger seat of the same Isetta.

Isettas have been seen all over the world. This well-travelled 1957 German-built example is seen here high in the Andes in 1960. Note the rock-strewn condition of what we assume is the road. The driver, Vic Locke, was with the British Diplomatic Service in Peru with his wife Hanny.

Harold Murray of Southport carried out this interesting conversion using Isetta three-wheeler components and a specially made body. What had become of the original body to bring about such a drastic course of action cannot be ascertained. The picture is thought to date from the mid-'60s. The presence of such a vehicle at a rally today would cause much consternation among the purists, but it surely demonstrates skill and ingenuity on the part of the owner, and ensures that at least one Isetta remained in service when it would otherwise have been scrapped.

The late Dan Sadwin (with cap and cigar) and his family used their Isetta for charity fund-raising events in Rhode Island, sometimes charging for rides, with the proceeds going to help the Jerry Lewis children's charity 'Jerry's Kids'. Here the year is 1985 and the Isetta is dressed up as a space shuttle. Leisa Sadwin (standing up through sun-roof – without beard!) was shortlisted for the 'Teacher in Space' project on the ill-fated Challenger flight, but in the event it was Christa McAuliffe who went on that tragic fatal mission.

A total of approximately 160,000 Isettas were made in Germany, including a small percentage with twin rear wheels set very close together for the Swiss market, plus 30,000 in Great Britain. With several thousand more from each of the other Isetta manufacturing countries the total was far higher than for any other microcar of the period. British production both started and finished later than most, with the final example leaving the Brighton works in 1964. More than thirty years on there is a lively and enthusiastic following for all models of Isetta, the world over.

Contrary to ill-informed opinion, it must be stated quite categorically that the Messerschmitt was not made from left-over fighter aircraft with the wings cut off. In fact, the Messerschmitt bubble car has its roots in transport for disabled war veterans, rather humbler than fighter aircraft yet far more humanitarian. Various types appeared, some of the first with manual propulsion, but later models progressing to small petrol engines, many the work of designer Fritz Fend. Eventually these primitive vehicles evolved into the Fend Flitzer, of which the Messerschmitt bubble car was the direct descendant.

The Flitzer proved a success. Fend's limited production facilities were stretched, and it was obvious that if he was to develop his machine into a commercially viable mode of transport he would need the help of an established industrialist. He approached Willi Messerschmitt, who still had the remnants of his aircraft manufacturing empire but was prohibited under the terms of Germany's 1945 defeat from making aeroplanes. Thus was eventually born the almost inevitable outcome – the Messerschmitt bubblecar, an early example of which is shown here.

Realistically, the makers avoided referring to the Messerschmitt as a car, preferring instead the term *Kabine-Roller* – literally cabin-scooter. Although a prototype powered by a 150 cc engine was built, the KR 175 with a single-cylinder Fichtel & Sachs engine of 174 cc was the first production model, and could lay claim to being the first real bubble-car with its now familiar clear plastic dome top.

Controls within the cockpit of the KR 175 displayed a marked similarity to those found on motorcycles, with handlebar steering and twist-grip throttle. However, gear selection was by a hand lever mounted at the side, and a handbrake was situated adjacent to the driver's left shin. Footbrake and clutch pedals followed car practice. The windscreen wipers were hand operated from the start, but electrification of this useful component soon followed.

The tandem seating arrangement endowed the Kabine-scooter with stability but luggage space was at a premium. The solution, a rack on the right-hand side of the vehicle, may have been slightly detrimental to the aforementioned stability, but offered a useful compromise.

Following its debut at the Geneva Show of March 1953, and in spite of representing so radical a concept, the Messerschmitt proved to be an instant success, with sales not only on the home market but overseas. Because trading restrictions obstructed the marketing of the German Messerschmitt in Italy, a licence to build a version with an engine of their own manufacture was granted to the Italian Mi-Val company, who had been making motorcycles since 1950, and who christened their new baby the MiValino. This illustration comes from an original Swedish market Messerschmitt brochure.

With its revolutionary design, the Messerschmitt certainly caught the attention of the world. Generically it occupied a position somewhere between the smart new Italian scooters and the minicar . . . a position that had not previously seemed to exist. The Messerschmitt had a style of its own, and was the precursor to many subsequent makes and models of microcar. Perhaps most oddly, the top opened by swinging upwards on a side hinge, so that drivers in its native country (and elsewhere in the left-hand-drive world) were forced to alight into the road, rather than on to the pavement.

In most respects the KR 175, also called the Cruisette, established design practice that was followed by all subsequent Messerschmitts, but certain features that were soon engineered out included the manual windscreen wiper and a mechanically engaged reversing system, although this was not normally supplied to British customers anyway, many of whom were only licensed to drive motorcycles, which class of licence included tricycles only if devoid of a means of reversing. Suspension was provided at the front by rubber mountings, and a large coil spring beneath the driving seat cushioned the driver against the worst road shocks. Production of the KR 175 lasted for two years, during which time nearly 20,000 examples were built. A range of extras became available, the list including 'spare wheel, chrome-plated hub caps, clock, canvas pocket for removable lateral windows, special-type car radio (6 circuits, 5 valves), sun blind', and of course that side-mounted luggage rack.

February 1955 saw the launch of the new KR 200 model, incorporating many improvements. Visually the most important changes were the all new wrap-around windscreen and wheelarch cut-aways to allow for an increase in track, which in turn allowed for new rubber-in-torsion suspension with telescopic dampers. Early KR 200 models retained the louvres in the top of the tail for about six months. The engine was an all new Fichtel & Sachs two-stroke single of 191 cc – hence the 200 designation – producing 10.2 ps.

A host of improvements could be found within the KR 200 cabin. New seating arrangements meant that a child could be seated next to an adult passenger at the rear, or alternatively the child seat could be raised and the space used for luggage. A pocket for maps was incorporated in the back of the driving seat. The sides were fully fitted with liners, and another pocket was convenient for the driver's right hand. For enhanced driver comfort, a new moulded plastic-covered steering bar became the norm. With all these new features it was not surprising that sales of the last few KR 175 models had to be encouraged by discounts and other incentives.

This was a period of change for the whole world. Notice how Great Britain had lost an Empire but gained a Commonwealth since the previous advertisement.

'Export' (De Luxe in Great Britain) KR 200 models came with the option of two-tone paintwork, at first having the secondary colour applied below an aluminium moulding along the bottom of the body, and later simply having the front wings in a contrasting colour. A comprehensive range of extras continued to be offered, both by the makers and as after-market add-ons. The tubular assembly shown here resembling a towel rail could be deemed to be the forerunner of the 'bull bar', though the term seems a little inappropriate here. This accessory was found only in North America, where this picture was taken at a show in 1996.

Although the KR 200 had been well received by press and public alike, Fend felt the need to further prove the model's capabilities, and to attract still more attention. A special KR 200 was built based upon the standard vehicle and components, but clad in a wind-cheating aerodynamic body. The engine output was increased to 13 ps. This car was driven for twenty-four hours at the Hockenheimring on 29 August 1955, breaking many existing records, and establishing many more that have yet to be surpassed, including an average over the entire twenty-four hours of 66.5 mph.

During 1956 Messerschmitt, in anticipation of a return to aircraft manufacture, had been seeking a way out of microcar production. The last of 20,840 true Messerschmitt KR 200s left the assembly line during December of that year. As from January 1957 production was transferred to Fahrzeug und Maschinebau GMBH Regensburg, and initially continued unchanged except for the vehicle identity plate attached to each car. Gradually, though, FMR established their own identity. Following protests from Daimler-Benz, the 'Messerschmitt Eagle' emblem was dropped – apparently it resembled the Mercedes three-pointed star too closely. However, brochures using the old photography continued to show this badge on the car.

The new emblem with three interlocking circles framing the letters FMR that had been chosen also became the subject of protests. Apparently this one was too similar to the four interlocking circles of the Auto-Union badge. The circles were changed to diamonds, and honour was satisfied all round.

A new Roadster model, the KR 201, was introduced early in 1957. This was similar to the KR 200 in most respects, but in place of the fully enclosing dome it just had a windscreen. A folding hood with expanding frame was fitted for weather protection, and flexible side curtains were provided. Snake-skin effect interior trim became a special option. The FMR KR 200 range was moving up market, and at the end of 1957 the Standard model was abandoned.

A further variation, the Cabriolet, appeared in the autumn of 1958. This was little different from the usual cabin type, but in place of the 'Plexiglass' acrylic dome it was fitted with an interchangeable roll-back hood on the same frame. In later years, when Messerschmitts and other bubble cars were the accepted transport of the young and impoverished, these soft-tops became more popular as relatively inexpensive replacements for the vulnerable domes.

With its sporty fun-car image the Messerschmitt proved to be 'media friendly', and began to appear in photographs with all manner of celebrities. This early cabriolet has comedy actor Sid James in the front seat, clearly enjoying the attentions of his back-seat driver. Perhaps the parking restriction was waived for the occasion.

WOU 176, a 1959 KR 200 then owned by the author's mother, was used in a comedy film called *Side By Side*, made at Shepperton Studios in 1975. The film also starred Terry-Thomas, Barry Humphries and a selection of long-forgotten lesser personalities. The story called for the car to go out of control down a steep embankment (actually the construction site for the junction of the M25 and M3 motorways. A 'double' was used for this scene. Sadly the film proved to be something of a flop, seeming never to have achieved general release.

Production of the KR 200 range continued largely unchanged, though the engine power output was reduced from 10.2 to 9.7 ps, changes were made to the electrical system, and the interior was given a face-lift in 1959. In January 1964, by which time the microcar era was on the wane, manufacture came to an end. KR 200 and 201 production by FMR totalled 25,350.

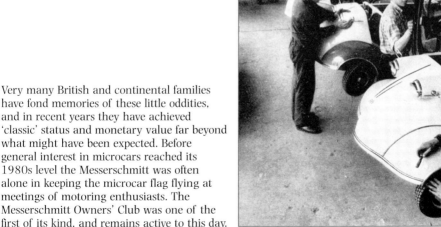

Very many British and continental families have fond memories of these little oddities, and in recent years they have achieved 'classic' status and monetary value far beyond what might have been expected. Before general interest in microcars reached its 1980s level the Messerschmitt was often alone in keeping the microcar flag flying at meetings of motoring enthusiasts. The Messerschmitt Owners' Club was one of the first of its kind, and remains active to this day.

Club trips have always been popular with the enthusiasts, and as the cars have become older, so their owners have become more ambitious. This shot, taken on 3 November 1974, shows fellow club members rallying round while Chris Lewis attends to a minor problem in Redhill, Surrey. Twenty-five years on, Messerschmitts joined other microcars on trips across Europe and far into the Arctic Circle. The white car on the pavement was to take part in the film *Side By Side* a few months after this shot was snapped.

Family transport: in about 1976 the author's brother made a trip in his KR200 (right) from Box Hill, Surrey, to Tunbridge Wells to purchase a lawnmower of a particular make and model. He was accompanied on the journey by his wife and their two small daughters. The lawnmower was duly purchased and the family brought it home with them in the Messerschmitt!

Often referred to as 'the ultimate in bubble cars', the FMR Tg 500 was developed from the KR200 design in 1957, but was a very different vehicle. Using the same basic body unit, it was powered by a special twin-cylinder two-stroke engine of 494 cc, with four forward speeds and reverse. To cope with the extra performance the brakes were enlarged and converted to hydraulic operation, which dictated that 10 inch wheels were to replace those of 8 inch diameter on the KR200 range. This, in turn, meant that the wings had to be enlarged. Larger headlamps were also incorporated. Originally destined to be called the Tiger, the name had to be dropped when it was found to have already been registered by another company, but four-wheeled Messerschmitts will always be regarded as Tigers.

With a top speed reputed to be approaching 90 mph, and acceleration to match, the Tiger was seldom photographed standing still. This picture appeared on manufacturer's publicity material.

The most famous exponent of Tiger racing and rallying was Ken Piper, who is seen in action on this page on his way to collecting a total of approximately forty cups. Only a handful of Tigers were imported to England commercially, and each one is now accounted for, most having survived. The last of just under 1,000 TG500s left the Regensburg factory at the beginning of 1964. A final batch of engines, however, later found their way to Australia, where they were used to power the Zeta Sports car made by the Lightburn Company.

It is not generally well known that the makers of the Messerschmitt were at one time considering the introduction of a more conventional small car. This model did not progress beyond the initial stages, leaving the world with the memory of a family of bubblecars whose evolution is illustrated by this group photograph of (right to left) Fend Flitzer, KR 175, KR 200, and TG 500. All these vehicles and many more are to be found at Automuseum Störy, in Germany.

CHAPTER NINE

MORE CAR THAN MICRO

From the beginning some manufacturers have placed their faith more in miniature cars of conventional appearance than in the weird and wonderful. Even a few of the very largest manufacturers made small cars that are considered to fall within the microcar category, most notably the Fiat 500 and 600 ranges, Citroën 2CV, and the pretty little NSU Prinz cars. In this section, though, we shall concentrate mainly, though not solely, on the products of Hans Glas GMBH, whose factory at Dingolfing, Bavaria, turned out many thousands of small cars bearing the brand name Goggomobil.

Fondly remembered and now eagerly sought by the enthusiast, Goggomobils soon found a niche in many export territories. Spanish-built derivatives catered for the Iberian market, and there was even a factory in Australia. Today the Dingolfing plant makes top-range BMW cars, and one wonders whether these, despite being excellent products, will become as much a part of their owners' families as did so many little Goggomobil saloons and coupés.

The Goggomobil has long been a favourite with microcar enthusiasts. In its day it was also one of the most successful in terms of sales, and of reliability. The company of Hans Glas GMBH had other interests before it became involved with cars, though, and had been producing motor-scooters with ILO engines of 123 cc, 148 cc, and 197 cc since 1951. In 1955 this prototype small car, called the Goggomobil T 250, was built. The result was sufficiently encouraging for the company to dispose of its scooter interests to the Tula company in the USSR, who continued manufacture under their own brand name.

The T 250 was a proper four-wheeled car in miniature. There were four forward-facing seats, and a twin-cylinder Glas two-stroke engine in a separate compartment at the back. There was one startlingly obvious difference between the prototype and production models: the entire front of the original opened for access in a manner similar to the Isetta, but with rear passengers then having to negotiate the tip-forward front seats en route to their own accommodation. As the rear seat was intended for children, who were usually more agile than their elders, this was considered acceptable.

By 1956, when production started, the car had evolved into the form which has since proved so durable. The whole shell had been redesigned with a more rounded appearance, and the opening front had been banished, to be replaced with more conventional, though rear-hinged, side doors. This made entry to the rear seat far easier, even if accommodation was still only really suitable for the *Kinder*. Isn't this typical? While mother fusses around little brother with father looking on benignly, older brother obviously has anxieties of his own. And just look at those fashions.

As with the Isetta, the domestic market was catered for with an engine of under 0.25 litre – actually 247 cc – fitted under the rear bonnet. This did little for performance, but made the car eligible for a special class which could be driven by under-age owners and with lower road tax. The standard model for Britain was the T 300, with 15 instead of 14 ps power available. By 1957 there were twin windscreen wipers, the doors had wind-up windows, and the model name Regent was adopted for the United Kingdom market.

With the Goggomobil saloon selling well, Glas surprised the world with a Coupé version for the 1957 season. With lines that have hardly dated in the intervening years, this model, the TS 300 or 400 depending upon engine size, named Mayfair in Britain, offered the sort of style that was so often missing from cars at the cheaper end of the market. It was not just about style, though. Mechanically similar to the saloons, the Coupé offered the option of a Getrag electro-magnetic pre-selector gearbox as original equipment. The TS 250, for the German market, did not have this refinement.

Goggomobil Coupés were normally supplied with two-tone paint finishes in a choice of colour combinations. The illustration shows how this feature was even extended to the interior trim. A very rare model in the range was a cabriolet, based on the Coupé bodyshell. Goggomobil saloons and Coupés remained in production for the German market for many years, the last not leaving the factory until about 1968, by which time the Glas company had been absorbed by BMW – whose name was displayed on the VIN plate.

Not content with making a huge impact in the small car field, Glas also built a commercial vehicle based upon the same mechanical units – even the Getrag pre-select gearbox was a possibility. The van offered a useful payload of 250 kg, and an impressive capacity for the carriage of bulky items. The sliding doors were useful for speedy entry and exit, and the German postal service was an enthusiastic user.

A further variant was introduced at the same time. The pick-up was fundamentally similar to the van, but the rear portion of the body was open with a drop-down tailboard. As with any commercial vehicle, these have survived less well than the cars, but they can still be seen at enthusiasts' meets in Germany and the Netherlands.

From 1961 Spanish manufacture of Goggomobil cars and commercial vehicles was transferred to Mungula Industrial SA of Bilbao. This photograph taken outside the Mungula premises shows a selection of Spanish Goggomobil products.

As stated earlier, the 247 cc Goggomobil was built mainly for the German market, where legislation encouraged cars with engines of less than 250 cc. Indeed, this very law was responsible for a curious situation after Glas production had ceased: Fiat 500s were stripped of their original engines and tiny reconditioned 250 cc Goggo units were installed as replacements! The AWS Shopper was a 1970s vehicle utilising Goggomobil parts. With a body structure built up from aluminium framing and flat panels, it showed little indication of its pedigree. However, underneath was a standard Goggomobil floorpan and engine. Wheels, lights, instruments and more were all Goggomobil-sourced.

The AWS Shopper was apparently the ideal leisure transport for Abba lookalikes, as demonstrated by this brochure illustration.

NEW! EXCITING GOGGO DART

FIRST REAL SPORTS CAR AT A PRICE YOU CAN AFFORD...

The Goggomobil 300 was the staple diet for most countries, with the 400 available for a bit of extra 'oomph', if that word can really be considered suitable. In Australia, though, Goggomobils were imported minus bodywork. This method of shipping allowed more to be packed into the holds, and also meant that they attracted a lower rate of import duty. Locally built fibreglass replicas of the genuine Glas bodies were fitted before the cars were supplied by the distributors, Buckle Motors of Sydney, New South Wales. Not only saloon bodies were made, but also coupé, and even commercial van, all largely indistinguishable from the steel bodies fitted to European cars. The fertile imagination of Bill Buckle, son of the company owner, conceived the idea of a small sports car based on the standard Goggomobil Coupé floorpan and mechanics. This car was given the model name Dart.

A design was sketched and passed to a local engineer, Stan Brown, who had been responsible for some impressive one-off racing cars. The result was a quite diminutive but undeniably pretty little car offering accommodation for two adults in the front with occasional seating for two in the rear. Weather protection in the form of a fabric hood and sidescreens was included in the specification. Originator Bill Buckle is seen here in the driving seat, obviously a happy man.

Approximately seven hundred Goggo Darts were sold in Australia, mostly in the doorless style shown, partly to simplify the manufacturing process and partly to create greater structural rigidity. However, a small proportion of the cars were to a slightly different design, with doors incorporated. There was even a factory hard-top that could be hinged back for easy access to the car. The Dart was unknown in the northern hemisphere until a used bodyshell arrived at the home of microcar enthusiast Malcolm Thomas in 1984. Since that time interest has grown, and at least one complete Goggo Dart was imported. British-made replica Dart bodyshells became available during 1998, of such good quality that the authenticity of the genuine product made by Buckle Motors between 1959 and 1961 may be difficult to establish.

The Dart seen above was photographed in 1983 with its owner Richard Cullen. In place of the original Glas rear lights Morris 1100 units have been substituted. It otherwise remains largely original more than twenty years after leaving the factory. The very curved windscreen so in keeping with the lines of the Dart was actually a Renault Dauphine rear screen.

The success of the Goggomobil and other microcars that were real cars in miniature focused the attention of other makers on that area of the market. Fiat, Lloyd, NSU and others were already established but newcomers included the Italian company of Piaggio, famous as creators of the Vespa Scooter, who joined the fray in 1957 with their pretty little Vespa 400 Coupé.

Although Vespa in name, all the 400s were actually made at Fourchambault, Nièvre, in the centre of France, by Ateliers de Constructions de Motos et Accessoires (usually abbreviated to ACMA). Only one model was made, sold in either Touring or the better equipped De Luxe versions. Both were two-seater cars with space for the accommodation of small children in the back. Comparison with a similar sized Goggomobil serves to emphasise the attractive styling of the Vespa.

The attractive Italian-styled steel body, not unlike the contemporary Autobianchi Bianchina (left), had a roll-back sun roof as standard equipment. The 393 cc two-stroke twin-cylinder engine was fitted at the rear, and transmission was by a three-speed and reverse gearbox with syncromesh on second and third. To save space the spare wheel (4.40 × 10 inch tyre size) was located in a well beneath the passenger seat, and the battery on a slide-out tray behind the front grille.

CHAPTER TEN

BORN TOO LATE

By the close of the 1950s it was apparent that the age of the microcar was on the wane. The world was changing rapidly, and with it people's aspirations and expectations. No longer was a low-powered engine of one or two cylinders thought sufficient. Microcars were regarded as funny-looking things that made a strange poppity-pop noise as they went along and left behind a blue exhaust haze. Most buyers now demanded cars that looked and sounded normal, with plenty of passenger and luggage space. Under the bonnet they expected to find multi-cylinder engines with filler caps for topping up lubricant and coolant. Never mind that all this cost more money – the world was enjoying spiralling growth and affluence.

The death knell was sounded on 18 August 1959, when pictures of the new Morris Mini-Minor appeared in the media. Microcars did not disappear overnight, though. Sales of some continued until the mid-1960s, while a very small minority did not even appear until the Mini had already become a feature of the everyday scene. One such was the BSA Ladybird.

The BSA motorcycle manufacturing concern commenced production of a motor scooter offered with the choice of BSA Sunbeam or Triumph Tigress identities in 1958. Both models were available with either a 175 cc single-cylinder two-stroke or 250 cc ohv twin.

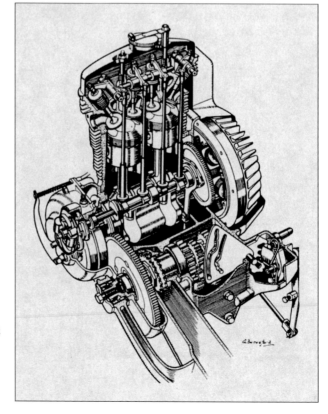

BSA chief Edward Turner considered several schemes for vehicles additional to the range that would further utilise the 250 cc engine design, one of these being a three-wheeled car. Designed at the Meriden works of BSA's Triumph subsidiary, and built by Carbodies Ltd, another BSA company, better known for the manufacture of taxicabs, the resulting prototype became known as the Ladybird.

The first Ladybird prototype featured a very simple hand-made steel body with open-top and rear-mounted engine. A hinged hatch on the top surface of the tail allowed access for minor maintenance. Steering was by a crescent-shaped handlebar. With an anticipated price of approximately £285 for the car the specification did not encompass such extras as windscreen wiper or direction indicators, with which items the Triumph motorcycle designers would in any case have been unfamiliar.

The car was retained for a while by BSA, but its condition deteriorated with bits and pieces being cannibalised for other projects. The car underwent restoration in the United States after it was acquired by Vic Hyde, an American entertainer with a penchant for microcars.

Subsequently repatriated to England and restored to as-new condition, Ladybird 1 has attended a number of rallies and has even been seen on television.

Interest in the Ladybird project was sufficient for a second prototype to be deemed desirable. This improved version differed from the original in having a removable hinged hard-top and twin windscreen wipers. The restyled tail had a flat rear panel, air intake scoops at the sides, and a larger maintenance hatch. The steering control was changed from the curved bar of the earlier car, and now formed a segment resembling the top third of a circle. Direction indicators were still not fitted.

The fate of Ladybird 2 has yet to be discovered, with suggestions that it was last heard of in the ownership of a mysterious Mr Hitchcock of Folkestone so far unfounded. While the BSA Sunbeam/Triumph Tigress scooters continued in production until 1962, the Ladybird project was abandoned by BSA in about 1960, when it became evident that the golden age of the microcar was over. (Photos: the late I.G. Davies)